INSTANT INFORMATION ON THE INTERNET!

A Genealogist's No-Frills Guide to

THE 50 STATES & THE DISTRICT OF COLUMBIA

CHRISTINA K. SCHAEFER

Published by Genealogical Publishing Co., Inc.
1001 N. Calvert St., Baltimore, Md. 21202
Second printing 1999
Library of Congress Catalogue Card Number 98-75655
International Standard Book Number 0-8063-1608-X
Made in the United States of America

For my son, Eric

CONTENTS

INTRODUCTION

Instant Information on the Internet! is designed to guide the researcher to the most important sites on the Internet, giving the addresses (URLs) of the best web sites for genealogical research in each of the fifty states and the District of Columbia. It tells how and where to locate records, contact other researchers, exchange information, and locate indexes that can be searched free of charge on a home computer. Designed specifically for speed and convenience, *Instant Information on the Internet!* provides immediate access to the top tier of genealogy resources on the Internet and is the logical starting point for genealogical research in this promising new medium.

Instant Information on the Internet! is organized by state. Under each state is listed, in the following order:

1. The state department of vital records. Although electronic ordering is offered only by some states, many state sites offer printable forms for mail ordering vital records.
2. The state archives, historical society, and library. Sometimes these functions are combined under the auspices of one institution.
3. Any National Archives Records Centers located within the state.
4. In alphabetical order, other state, regional, and local archives, libraries, museums, societies, and other resources.
5. A section of information sites, listing how-to information, state history, and so forth.
6. A selection of indexes (some as lists, some in searchable databases) and documents and publications in digitized form.
7. Sites containing links to other sites, and lists of addresses of important genealogical resources.

The various state agencies responsible for maintaining, archiving, and preserving original records among the states are similar in function, but can vary greatly in name. There has been a trend to amalgamate the functions under the title "Department of Archives and History," as is the case with Alabama and Georgia. Some states, such as Iowa and Kansas, maintain an archive as a division of the state historical society. In other states, the historical society may be a privately-endowed institution and not a department of state government. Yet still, some states, such as Connecticut and Virginia, use the institution of the state library as a records repository.

A few of the geographically-disparate states, such as Minnesota, Ohio, Washington, and Wisconsin, have established area or regional centers, making use of state and private college and university libraries. Many of these centers contain large microform collections, enabling researchers to avoid traveling great distances to examine census and other records. Arizona maintains several divisions of its historical society, facilitating specialization and focus in the acquisition of local and regional collections.

Readily found in most state archive, library, college, and university Internet sites are online catalogs. This is especially exciting for the genealogist, as it can open up a new world of possibilities of published and secondary source material. Some archives and universities also maintain databases of their archival collections, and they can be searched by subject.

The only state historical societies that do not presently maintain a web site are the Rhode Island State Historical Society in Providence and the New Jersey Historical Society in Newark (a site is under construction). The only "state" archives not online is the District of Columbia Archives. There are very few **gopher** sites listed in this book: of the major repositories, only the Rhode Island State Archives maintains a **gopher** site, although an **http** is reportedly under construction.

There are several ways to gain general access to a U.S. state on the Internet. The easiest way is through the state governments online. Their URL addresses are all written **http://www.state.**.us/**, and you must substitute the two-letter postal abbreviation for **, such as **http://www.state.al.us/** for Alabama, **http://www.state.il.us/** for Illinois, and so forth. The US GenWeb Project home page has links for all of its state home pages, as do most of the other genealogical sites, such as Roots-L and ListServ.

I have visited every site listed in this book, and all addresses are current as of the time of publication. Fortunately, sites are becoming more stable, and if they do change they will continue to forward the user to the new site, at least for a few months. Please also note that the abbreviation FHL stands for the Family History Library of the Church of Jesus Christ of Latter-day Saints.

As a dedicated bibliophile, I favor published guides to accompany any research endeavor so I can plan in advance what needs to be done and the order in which I want to do it. With the fast and furious pace of cyber information, it is still a good idea to leave a paper trail. *Instant Information on the Internet!* helps pinpoint on the Internet not only where information can be found, but how to backtrack and reconstruct what has already been searched.

My thanks go to Michael Tepper and Eileen Perkins at Genealogical Publishing Company. I would also like to give a special hats-off to Marthe Arends, author of *Genealogy Software Guide* (Baltimore: Genealogical Publishing Co., 1998) and my technical editor, who taught me *anything* I know about working smart on the Internet.

Happy Hunting!

ALABAMA

Alabama Department of Public Health, Center for Health Statistics, Montgomery
www.alapubhealth.org/frames2.htm

Alabama Department of Archives and History (ADAH), Montgomery
www.asc.edu/archives/agis.html

Birmingham Public Library, Department of Archives and Manuscripts
www.bham.lib.al.us/departments/archives/archives.html

Huntsville-Madison County Public Library, Huntsville
www.hpl.lib.al.us/departments/hhr

Mobile Public Library
www2.acan.net/~mplhp/index.html

Northeast Alabama Genealogical Society, Gadsen
www.geocities.com/Heartland/Ranch/5952

Samford University Library, Birmingham
davisweb.samford.edu/

Tennessee Valley Genealogical Society, Huntsville
hiwaay.net/~white/TVGS/tvgs.html

University of Alabama, W.S. Hoole Special Collections Library, Tuscaloosa
www.lib.ua.edu/

INFORMATION SITES

ADAH Newspapers on Film, by County
www.asc.edu/archives/newsp/newsp.html

ADAH Vital Records on Film
www.asc.edu/archives/referenc/vital.html

ADAH Collection of County Records
www.asc.edu/archives/referenc/procount.html

ADAH African American Research
www.asc.edu/archives/afro/afro.html

SELECTED INDEXES AND DOCUMENTS ONLINE

Alabama Baptist Index
library.samford.edu/gateway02/english/

Bureau of Land Management Land Patent Records Site
www.glorecords.blm.gov/

Marriages of Alabama Index (grooms)
www.geocities.com/Heartland/Valley/6247/algrm1.html#anchor 38218

Marriages of Alabama Index (brides)
www.geocities.com/Heartland/Valley/6247/albrd1.html#anchor 38218

LISTS AND LINKS

*Alabama GenWeb Project
www.rootsweb.com/~algenweb/

*Genealogy Mailing Lists for Alabama
members.aol.com/gfsjohnf/gen_mail_states-al.html

*NUCMC Guide to Alabama Archives and Repositories
lcweb.loc.gov/coll/nucmc/alsites.html

*Tracking Your Roots (Alabama)
members.aol.com/GenWebLisa/tyralachart.htm

———— ••◦●◦•• ————

ALASKA

Department of Health and Social Services, Bureau of Vital Statistics, Anchorage
health.hss.state.ak.us/dph/bvs/bvs_home.htm

*Alaska Division of Archives, Libraries, and Museums
www.educ.state.ak.us/lam/lamalpha.html

Alaska State Library, Alaska Historical Collections, Juneau
www.educ.state.ak.us/lam/library/hist/hist.html

National Archives - Pacific Alaska Region (Anchorage)
www.nara.gov/regional/anchorag.html

University of Alaska Fairbanks, Elmer E. Rasmuson Library
www.uaf.alaska.edu/library/

INFORMATION SITES

Alaska Genealogy
www.educ.state.ak.us/lam/library/is/akgene.html

Alaska Newspaper Project
www.educ.state.ak.us/lam/library/hist/newspaper.html

How to Find Your Gold Rush Relative: Sources on the Klondike and
    Alaska Gold Rushes
www.educ.state.ak.us/lam/library/hist/parham.html

Villages in Alaska That Have Been Given Tribal Status
www.narf.org/resource/guide/states/ak.htm

SELECTED INDEXES AND DOCUMENTS ONLINE

Pan for Gold Database: Women of the Golden North Fraternal
    Organization
www.gold-rush.org/pan/gol_norb.htm

Rasmuson Library Oral History Index
www.elmer.alaska.edu/osearch.html

LISTS AND LINKS

*Alaska GenWeb Project
www.rootsweb.com/~akgenweb/

Alaska Library Directory
www.alaska.net/~akla/libdir.html

*Genealogy Mailing Lists for Alaska
members.aol.com/gfsjohnf/gen_mail_states-ak.html

*Museums and Historical Societies in Alaska
www.educ.state.ak.us/lam/museum/list.html

*NUCMC Guide to Alaska Archives and Repositories
lcweb.loc.gov/coll/nucmc/aksites.html

ARIZONA

Arizona Department of Health, Phoenix
www.hs.state.az.us/plan/ohpes.htm

Department of Library, Archives, and Public Records, Archives Division,
     Phoenix
www.lib.az.us/archives/

Arizona State Research Library, Phoenix
www.lib.az.us/research.htm

Arizona Historical Society, Central Arizona Division, Tempe
www.tempe.gov/ahs

Arizona Historical Society, Northern Arizona Division, Flagstaff
www.azstarnet.com/~azhist/divisions.htm

Arizona Historical Society, Rio Colorado Division, Yuma
www.tempe.gov/ahs/yuma.htm

Arizona Historical Society, Southern Arizona Division, Tucson
www.azstarnet.com/~azhist/

Arizona State Genealogical Society, Tucson
www.rootsweb.com/~asgs/

Arizona State University, Hayden Memorial Library, Arizona Historical
     Foundation, Tempe
www.asu.edu/lib/ahf/

Family History Society of Arizona, Phoenix
www.fhsa.org/

Phoenix Public Library, Arizona Room
www.ci.phoenix.az.us/library.html

University of Arizona, Tucson, Arizona State Museum Library
w3.arizona.edu:180/asm/drsw/index_dr.html

INFORMATION SITES

Accessing Arizona Public Records
www.lib.az.us/records/access.htm

Arizona Newspaper Project
www.lib.az.us/research/c-news.htm

Inventories of Arizona County Records
www.dlapr.lib.az.us/archives/local.htm

SELECTED INDEXES AND DOCUMENTS ONLINE

Arizona Genealogical Society Database
www.rootsweb.com/~asgs/nindex.html

LISTS AND LINKS

*Arizona GenWeb Project
www.rootsweb.com/~azgenweb/

*Genealogy Mailing Lists for Arizona
members.aol.com/gfsjohnf/gen_mail_states-az.html

*NUCMC Guide to Arizona Archives and Repositories
lcweb.loc.gov/coll/nucmc/azsites.html

ARKANSAS

Arkansas Department of Health, Division of Vital Records, Little Rock
health.state.ar.us/

Arkansas History Commission, Little Rock
www.state.ar.us/ahc/index.htm

Arkansas State Library, Little Rock
www.asl.lib.ar.us/

Department of Arkansas Heritage, Little Rock
www.heritage.state.ar.us/dah_serv.html

Arkansas Genealogical Society, Hot Springs
www.rootsweb.com/~args/

Arkansas State University Museum, Jonesboro
www.astate.edu/docs/admin/museum/index.htm

Arkansas Territorial Restoration, Little Rock
www.heritage.state.ar.us/atr/her_atr.html

Fort Smith Public Library, Arkansas Collection, Fort Smith
www.fspl.lib.ar.us/

Southwest Arkansas Regional Archives, Washington
www.gorp.com/gorp/location/ar/parks/old.htm

University of Arkansas at Fayetteville Library
cavern.uark.edu/libinfo.speccoll/

INFORMATION SITES

Guide to Genealogical Research in Arkansas
www.rootsweb.com/~usgenweb/ar/guide/

SELECTED INDEXES AND DOCUMENTS ONLINE

*Arkansas Biographies
www.rootsweb.com/~usgenweb/ar/biography/bios-ark1.htm

Bureau of Land Management Land Patent Records Site
www.glorecords.blm.gov/

LISTS AND LINKS

*Arkansas GenWeb Project
bl-12.rootsweb.com/~argenweb/

*Arkansas Links
www.uark.edu/libinfo/arkres/index.html

*Genealogy Mailing Lists for Arkansas
members.aol.com/gfsjohnf/gen_mail_states-ar.html

*NUCMC Guide to Arkansas Archives and Repositories
lcweb.loc.gov/coll/nucmc/arsites.html

*Indicates URL with links to other sites

CALIFORNIA

Department of Health Services, Office of Vital Records, Sacramento
www.cdc.gov/nchswww/howto/w2w/californ.htm

California State Archives, Sacramento
www.ss.ca.gov/archives/archives.htm

California State Library, Sacramento
www.library.ca.gov/

California State Library, Sutro Library Branch, San Francisco
sfpl.lib.ca.us/gencoll/gencolsu.htm

California Historical Society Library, San Francisco
www.calhist.org/

National Archives—Pacific Region (Laguna Niguel)
www.nara.gov/regional/laguna.html

National Archives—Pacific Region (San Francisco)
www.nara.gov/regional/sanfranc.html

California Genealogical Society, San Francisco
pw2.netcom/~dwilma/cgs.html

Genealogical and Historical Council of the Sacramento Valley,
      Sacramento
calgensoc.com/

Henry E. Huntington Library, San Marino
www.huntington.org/LibraryDiv/LibraryHome.html

Los Angeles Public Library, History and Genealogy Department
www.lapl.org/central/hihp.html

National Maritime Museum and Library, San Francisco
www.maritime.org/

National Japanese American Historical Society, San Francisco
www.nikkeiheritage.org/main.html

Southern California Genealogical Society, Burbank
www.cwire.com/scgs/

Stanford University, Special Collections, Stanford
www-sul.stanford.edu/depts/spc

University of California Berkeley, Bancroft Library
www.lib.berkeley.edu/BANC/

University of California Santa Barbara, Ethnic and Multicultural
  Archives
www.library.ucsb.edu/speccoll/cemabro.html

INFORMATION SITES

California Pioneer Project
www.compuology.com/cpl/

County Records on Film at the State Archives and at the FHL
www.ss.ca.gov/archives/level3_county.htm

Genealogy Sources at the California State Library
www.library.ca.gov/html/genealogy.html

San Francisco Public Library Genealogy Page
sfpl.lib.ca.us/gencoll/gencolgn.htm

SELECTED INDEXES AND DOCUMENTS ONLINE

California Counties Biographical Index
www.compuology.com/cpl/cpl_bio.htm

LISTS AND LINKS

*California GenWeb Project
www.compuology.com/cagenweb/

*Genealogy Mailing Lists for California
members.aol.com/gfsjohnf/gen_mail_states-ca.html

*NUCMC Guide to California Archives and Repositories
lcweb.loc.gov/coll/nucmc/casites.html

COLORADO

Colorado Department of Health Statistics, Vital Records Division, Denver
www.state.co.us/gov_dir/cdphe_dir/hs/hshom.html

Colorado State Archives, Denver
www.state.co.us/gov_dir/gss/archives/arcother.html

Colorado Historical Society, Denver
www.aclin.org/other/historic/chs

National Archives—Rocky Mountain Region (Colorado)
www.nara.gov/regional/denver.html

Boulder Public Library, Carnegie Branch for Local History
www.bldr.net/carnegie

Colorado Genealogical Society, Denver
www.cogensoc.org/cgs/cgs-home.htm

Denver Public Library, Genealogy Division
www.denver.lib.co.us/

Fort Collins Public Library, Local History Archive
library.ci.fort-collins.co.us/

Fort Lewis College, Center for Southwest Studies, Durango
www.fortlewis.edu/acad-aff/swcenter

Southeastern Colorado Genealogical Society, Inc., Pueblo
members.aol.com/annray5543/private/Local.html

INFORMATION SITES

Marriage Records at the State Archives
webdig01.state.co.us/gov_dir/gss/archives/marr1.html

Naturalization Records at the State Archives
www.state.co.us/gov_dir/gss/archives/natural.html

SELECTED INDEXES AND DOCUMENTS ONLINE

1861 Territorial Election Books
[no http:] **gopher://dpl20.denver.lib.co.us:70/11/genealogy/Colorado %20Resources/Colorado%201862%20Territorial%20Election**

Colorado Civil War Casualties
www.state.co.us/gov_dir/gss/archives/ciwardea.html

Colorado Civil War Volunteers Index, 1861–1865
www.state.co.us/gov_dir/gss/archives/trans/home.html

Colorado Marriage and Divorce Index, 1890–1939, 1975–1996
www.state.co.us/gov_dir/cdphe_dir/hs/search.html

Colorado Veterans' Grave Registrations, 1862–1949
www.state.co.us/gov_dir/gss/archives/grave_dir/cograv.html

Reformatory Convict Index, 1887–1939
[no http:] **gopher://dpl20.denver.lib.co.us:70/11/genealogy/Colorado %20Resources/Colorado%20State%20Reformatory%20Prisoner%20 Records**

LISTS AND LINKS

*Colorado GenWeb Project
www.rootsweb.com/~cogenweb/comain.htm

*Genealogy Mailing Lists for Colorado
members.aol.com/gfsjohnf/gen_mail_states-co.html

*Links to Colorado Cities
www.state.co.us/communities_dir/communities.html

*NUCMC Guide to Colorado Archives and Repositories
lcweb.loc.gov/coll/nucmc/cosites.html

CONNECTICUT

Department of Public Health, Hartford
www.state.ct.us/dph/vr-birth.html

Connecticut State Library and Archives, Hartford
www.cslnet.ctstateu.edu/

Connecticut Historical Society, Hartford
www.hartnet.org/~chs/

Cyrenius Booth Library, Newtown
www.biblio.org/chbooth/chbooth.htm

Bridgeport Public Library Historical Collections
bridgeport.lib.ct.us/bpl/hc/hchp2.htm

Silas Bronson Library, Waterbury
www.biblio.org/bronson/silas.htm

Connecticut Society of Genealogists, East Hartford
www.knic.com/csg/

Godfrey Memorial Library, Middletown
www.godfrey.org/

Mashantucket Pequot Museum & Research Center, Mashantucket
www.mashantucket.com/

Mystic Seaport, Blunt White Library
mysticseaport.org/public/library/bluntlibrary.html

New Haven Colony Historical Society, New Haven
statlab.stat.yale.edu/cityroom/test/hist/loc_srcs/colony/index.html

Pequot Library, Southport
www.biblio.org/pequot/pequot.htm

University of Connecticut, Thomas J. Dodd Research Center, Storrs
www.lib.uconn.edu/DoddCenter/

Yale University, Beinecke Library, New Haven
www.library.yale.edu/beinecke/

INFORMATION SITES

Barbour and Hale Vital Records Collections Information
www.cslnet.ctstateu.edu/basic.htm

Guide to the New York, New Haven & Hartford Railroad Archives
www.lib.uconn.edu/DoddCenter/ASC/raillist.htm

Connecticut Newspaper Project
www.cslnet.ctstateu.edu/cnp.htm

SELECTED INDEXES AND DOCUMENTS ONLINE

Connecticut GenWeb Archives
www.rootsweb.com/~usgenweb/ct/ctfiles.htm

LISTS AND LINKS

*Connecticut GenWeb Project
www.99main.com/~jrothgeb/ctgenweb.htm

*Genealogy Mailing Lists for Connecticut
members.aol.com/gfsjohnf/gen_mail_states-ct.html

*NUCMC Guide to Connecticut Archives and Repositories
lcweb.loc.gov/coll/nucmc/ctsites.html

DELAWARE

Division of Public Health, Office of Vital Statistics, Dover
www.cdc.gov/nchswww/data/w2w5_98.pdf

*Delaware Public Archives, Hall of Records, Dover
www.lib.de.us/archives

*Historical Society of Delaware Library, Wilmington
www.hsd.org/

Delaware Genealogical Society, Wilmington
delgensoc.org/

Hagley Museum and Library, Greenville
www.hagley.lib.de.us/

University of Delaware Library, Newark
www.hsd.org/

12   ***Indicates URL with links to other sites**

Winterthur Museum and Library, Winterthur
www.winterthur.org/

INFORMATION SITES

*Directory of Historical Records in Delaware
www.lib.de.us/archives/dehisrec.htm

Vital Records in Delaware
lib.de.us/archives/vital.htm

SELECTED INDEXES AND DOCUMENTS ONLINE

Delaware GenWeb Archives
www.rootsweb.com/~usgenweb/de/defiles.htm

LISTS AND LINKS

*Delaware GenWeb Project
www.geocities.com/Heartland/8074/state_de.htm

*Genealogy Mailing Lists for Delaware
members.aol.com/gfsjohnf/gen_mail_states-de.html

*NUCMC Guide to Delaware Archives and Repositories
lcweb.loc.gov/coll/nucmc/desites.html

——————— ••●●●•• ———————

DISTRICT OF COLUMBIA

District of Columbia Vital Records Division
www.ci.washington.dc.us/HEALTH/vital.htm

District of Columbia Archives
[no Internet access, phone 202-727-2054]

Historical Society of Washington, DC
www.wam.umd.edu/~pbowen/welcome.htm

National Archives
www.nara.gov/

Library of Congress
lcweb.loc.gov

Catholic University, Mullen Library
www.cua.edu/libraries/archcoll.html

Georgetown University, Lauinger Library
gulib.lausun.georgetown.edu/dept/speccoll/

Martin Luther King Memorial Library, Washingtoniana Division
dconline.vais.net/html/divisions.htm#14

National Museum of American History Library, Smithsonian Institution
www.si.edu/organiza/museums/nmah/archives/ac-i.htm

National Society of the Daughters of the American Revolution
www.dar.org/

U.S. Holocaust Memorial Museum
www.ushmm.org/

INFORMATION SITES

Nidiffer Collection of Washington, DC Deeds
gulib.lausun.georgetown.edu/dept/speccoll/c196.htm

*Tips for Researchers in the District of Columbia
www.rootsweb.com/~dcgenweb/dctips.html

SELECTED INDEXES AND DOCUMENTS ONLINE

National Archives Information Locator (NAIL)
www.nara.gov/nara/nail.html

LISTS AND LINKS

*District of Columbia GenWeb Project
www.rootsweb.com/~dcgenweb

*Genealogy Mailing Lists for the District of Columbia
members.aol.com/gfsjohnf/gen_mail_states-dc.html

*NUCMC Guide to District of Columbia Archives and Repositories
lcweb.loc.gov/coll/nucmc/dcsites.html

FLORIDA

Florida Department of Health, Jacksonville
www.state.fl.us/health/

Florida State Archives, Tallahassee
www.dos.state.fl.us/dlis/barm/fsa.html

State Library of Florida, Tallahassee
stafla.dlis.state.fl.us/

Florida Historical Society, Tebeau-Field Library of Florida History, Cocoa
www.florida-historical-soc.org/teblib.htm

East Central Florida Genealogical Society, Tallahassee
www.rootsweb.com/~flecfgsc/

Florida State Genealogical Society, Tallahassee
www.rootsweb.com/~flsgs/

Historical Museum of Southern Florida Research Center, Miami
www.historical-museum.org/collect/rc.htm

Orlando Public Library
www.ocls.lib.fl.us/

Saint Augustine Historical Society and Research Library
www.oldcity.com/oldhouse/

University of Florida, P.K. Yonge Library of Florida History, Gainesville
special.uflib.ufl.edu/pkyonge/

University of West Florida, John Pace Library, Pensacola
www.lib.uwf.edu/HomePage/Departments/SpecCol/sp-col.htm

West Florida Genealogical Society, Pensacola
www.rootsweb.com/~flescamb/wfgs.htm

INFORMATION SITES

Chronology of Florida History
special.uflib.ufl.edu/pkyonge/chronol0.html

Family Histories at the Tebeau-Field Library of Florida History
www.rootsweb.com/~flsgs/fhsgen.htm

*Genealogy Resources at the University of South Florida Library, Tampa
www.lib.usf.edu:80/spccoll/genea.html

SELECTED INDEXES AND DOCUMENTS ONLINE

Bureau of Land Management Land Patent Records Site
www.glorecords.blm.gov/

Florida Confederate Pension Application Files Index
www.dos.state.fl.us/dlis/barm/PensionIntroduction.htm

LISTS AND LINKS

*Florida GenWeb Project
www.rootsweb.com/~flgenweb/index.html

*Genealogy Mailing Lists for Florida
members.aol.com/gfsjohnf/gen_mail_states-fl.html

*NUCMC Guide to Florida Archives and Repositories
lcweb.loc.gov/coll/nucmc/flsites.html

GEORGIA

Georgia Department of Public Health, Atlanta
www.ph.dhr.state.ga.us/org/vitalrecords.htm

Georgia Department of Archives and History, Atlanta
www.sos.state.ga.us/archives/

Georgia Historical Society Library, Savannah
www.savannah-online.com/ghs/

Atlanta History Center Library/Archives
www.atlhist.org/ahslibr.htm

Central Georgia Genealogical Society
www.rootsweb.com/~gacggs

Emory University, Robert W. Woodruff Library, Atlanta
www.cc.emory.edu/LIB/schome.htm

Georgia Genealogical Society, Atlanta
www.america.net/~ggs/index.html

Mercer University, Georgia Baptist History Depository, Macon
cdsearch.mercer.edu/mainlib/special_collections/default.htm

Ellen Payne Odom Genealogy Library, Moultrie
www.firstct.com/fv/EPO.html

Southwest Georgia Genealogical Society
www.geocities.com/Heartland/Meadows/7746/swggs/

Southwest Georgia Regional Library, Genealogy Room, Bainbridge
www.decatur.public.lib.ga.us/

Thomasville Genealogical, History, and Fine Arts Library
www.rose.net/culture.htm

Washington Memorial Library, Macon
www.co.bibb.ga.us/library/G&H.htm

INFORMATION SITES

Documenting Family History in Georgia
www.sos.state.ga.us/archives/dfhg.htm

Genealogical Research at the Georgia Department of Archives and
   History
www.sos.state.ga.us/archives/reference.htm

Georgia Land Lotteries
www.sos.state.ga.us/archives/landlottery.htm

SELECTED INDEXES AND DOCUMENTS ONLINE

*Georgia Records Online
www.rootsweb.com/~gagenweb/records/records.htm

Index to Confederate Pension Applications
docuweb.gsu.edu/htbin/collection/colid=200 l 203

LISTS AND LINKS

*Georgia Archival Repositories
www.soga.org/gar.html

*Georgia GenWeb Project
www.rootsweb.com/~gagenweb/

*Genealogy Mailing Lists for Georgia
members.aol.com/gfsjohnf/gen_mail_states-ga.html

*NUCMC Guide to Georgia Archives and Repositories
lcweb.loc.gov/coll/nucmc/gasites.html

HAWAII

State of Hawaii Department of Health, Honolulu
www.hawaii.gov/health/vr_howto.htm

Hawaii State Archives, Honolulu
kumu.icsd.hawaii.gov/dags/archives

Hawaiian Historical Society Library, Honolulu
www.flex.com/~mem/libmain.html

Bernice Pauahi Bishop Museum Library, Honolulu
www.bishop.hawaii.org/bishop/library/library.html

Hawaiian Mission Children's Society Library, Honolulu
www.hcc.hawaii.edu/artweb/mission/mission.html

University of Hawaii at Manoa, Hawaiian Collection
nic2.hawaii.edu/~speccoll/hawaii.html

INFORMATION SITES

Hawaiian Genealogy Resources
www.hawaii.gov/health/vr_gene.htm

Operation Ohana (registry of people with Hawaiian ancestry)
www.oha.org/index.html

SELECTED INDEXES AND DOCUMENTS ONLINE

Hawaiian Newspaper Genealogy, 1868
nic2.hawaii.edu/~speccoll/genealogy/hoahalahala.gif

Pearl Harbor Casualty List
ftp.rootsweb.com/pub/usgenweb/hi/military/pearl.txt

Portuguese Immigration to Hawaii, 1878–1913
ftp.rootsweb.com/pub/usgenweb/hi/shiplists/portug.txt

LISTS AND LINKS

*Genealogy Mailing Lists for Hawaii
members.aol.com/gfsjohnf/gen_mail_states-hi.html

*Hawaii GenWeb Project
www.rootsweb.com/~higenweb/hawaii.htm

Hawaii State Public Libraries
www.hcc.hawaii.edu/hspls/dirlibs.html

*NUCMC Guide to Hawaii Archives and Repositories
lcweb.loc.gov/coll/nucmc/hisites.html

*Pacific Studies
sunsite.anu.edu.au/spin/wwwvl-pacific/index.html

IDAHO

Center for Vital Statistics and Health Policy, Vital Statistics Unit, Boise
www.cdc.gov/nchswww/data/w2w5_98.pdf

Idaho State Historical Society, Boise
www2.state.id.us:80/ishs/

Idaho State Library, Boise
www.lili.org/isl/hp.htm

Idaho State University, Eli M. Oboler Library, Pocatello
www.isu.edu/library/home.htm

Ricks College, McKay Library Family History Center, Rexburg
abish.ricks.edu/fhc/fhchome.asp

University of Idaho Library, Moscow
www.uidaho.edu/

INFORMATION SITES

1895 Atlas of Idaho Towns
www.livgenmi.com/1895id

Idaho Genealogy
www.lib.uidaho.edu/special-collections/genealgl.htm

SELECTED INDEXES AND DOCUMENTS ONLINE

Idaho Marriage Database
www.rootsweb.com/~idgenweb/vital.htm

LISTS AND LINKS

*Genealogy Mailing Lists for Idaho
members.aol.com/gfsjohnf/gen_mail_states-id.html

*Idaho GenWeb Project
www.rootsweb.com/~idgenweb/

*Idaho Links
www2.state.id.us/HOME/OTHER/orgs.html

*NUCMC Guide to Idaho Archives and Repositories
lcweb.loc.gov/coll/nucmc/idsites.html

––––––– ••••◉••• –––––––

*Indicates URL with links to other sites

ILLINOIS

Illinois Department of Health, Springfield
www.idph.state.il.us/

Illinois State Archives, Springfield
www.sos.state.il.us/depts/archives/arc_home.html

Illinois Regional Archives Depository (IRAD), Springfield
www.sos.state.il.us/depts/archives/data_loc.html

Illinois State Library, Springfield
www.sos.state.il.us/depts/library/isl_home.html

Illinois State Historical Library, Springfield
www.state.il.us/hpa/lib/libpg.htm

Illinois State Historical Society, Springfield
www.prairienet.org/ishs/

National Archives—Great Lakes Region (Chicago)
www.nara.gov/regional/chicago.html

Augustana College, Center for Western Studies, Rock Island
inst.augie.edu/CWS/

Evangelical Lutheran Church in America Archives, Chicago
www.elca.org/os/archives/intro.html

Genealogy Society of Southern Illinois, Carterville
jal.cc.il.us/gssi.html

Illinois State Genealogical Society, Springfield
smtp.tbox.com/isgs/

Newberry Library, Chicago
www.newberry.org/

Polish Museum of America Library, Chicago
www.pgsa.org/

Tri-State Genealogical Society, Evansville, Indiana
www.evansville.net/~tsgs/tsgs.html

University of Illinois Urbana Library, Illinois Historical Survey
www.library.uiuc.edu/ihx/

INFORMATION SITES

Descriptive Inventory of the Archives of the State of Illinois. 2nd ed. (1997)
www.sos.state.il.us/depts/archives/di/toc.html

SELECTED INDEXES AND DOCUMENTS ONLINE

Bureau of Land Management Land Patent Records Site
www.glorecords.blm.gov/

Illinois Ancestor Registry
www.rootsweb.com/~ilgenweb/queries/

Illinois Civil War Veterans Database
www.sos.state.il.us/depts/archives/datcivil.html

Illinois Public Domain Land Tract Sales Database
www.sos.state.il.us/depts/archives/data_lan.html

Illinois Spanish-American War Veterans Database
www.sos.state.il.us/depts/archives/spanam.html

LISTS AND LINKS

*Genealogy Mailing Lists for Illinois
members.aol.com/gfsjohnf/gen_mail_states-il.html

*Illinois GenWeb Project
www.rootsweb.com/~ilgenweb/

*NUCMC Guide to Illinois Archives and Repositories
lcweb.loc.gov/coll/nucmc/ilsites.html

INDIANA

Indiana State Department of Health, Indianapolis
www.state.in.us/isdh/bdcertifs/birth_and_death_certificates.htm

Indiana State Archives, Indianapolis
www.ai.org/icpr/webfile/archives/homepage.html

Indiana State Library, Indiana Division, Indianapolis
www.statelib.lib.in.us/www/indiana/aboutind.html

Indiana Historical Society, Library Division, Indianapolis
www2.indianahistory.org/ihs1830/lib.htm

Allen County Public Library, Fort Wayne
www.acpl.lib.in.us/genealogy/genealogy.html

Batesville Memorial Public Library, Genealogy and Indiana History
www.bmpl.cnz.com/

Goshen College, Mennonite Historical Library, Goshen
www.goshen.edu/~lonhs/MHL.html

Indiana Genealogical Society, Fort Wayne
www.indgensoc.org/

Indiana University Library, Bloomington
www.indiana.edu/~libweb/mainlib.html

Indiana University-Purdue University at Fort Wayne, Helmke Library
www.lib.ipfw.edu/

Indiana University-Purdue University at Indianapolis, Lilly Archives
www-lib.iupui.edu/special/

Kokomo-Howard County Public Library, Genealogical and Local History
    Department, Kokomo
www.kokomo.lib.in.us/genealogy/

Monroe Public Library, Indiana Room Bloomington
www.monroe.lib.in.us/indiana_room/genealogy.html

Morgan County Public Library, Genealogy Section, Martinsville
www.scican.net/~morglib/genasist/genasist.html

Patrick Henry Sullivan Museum and Genealogy Library, Zionsville
www.artcom.com/museums/nv/mr/46077-16.htm

Ripley County Historical Society Library, Versailles
www.seidata.com/~rchslib/

Saint Joseph County Public Library, Local History and Genealogy, South Bend
www.sjcpl.lib.in.us/homepage/LocalHist/genealogy.html

Tri-State Genealogical Society, Evansville
www.evansville.net/~tsgs/tsgs.html

University of Notre Dame Archives, South Bend
archives1.archives.nd.edu/guidecon.htm

Vincennes University, Lewis Historical Library, Vincennes
www.vinu.edu/lewis.htm

Willard Library Regional and Family History Center, Evansville
www.willard.lib.in.us/

INFORMATION SITES

*Indiana Biographies Project
members.tripod.com/~debmurray/indybios/indiana1.htm

Indiana WPA Vital Records on Film
www.evansville.net/~tsgs/wpa_ndx.html

SELECTED INDEXES AND DOCUMENTS ONLINE

Bureau of Land Management Land Patent Records Site
www.glorecords.blm.gov/

Index of Marriages in County Records Through 1850
www.statelib.lib.in.us/www/indiana/genealogy/mirr.html

Indiana State Cemetery Database
www.statelib.lib.in.us/tango/marriage/cemetery.qry?function=form

General Land Office Records Database at the State Archives
www.state.in.us/icpr/webfile/land/general_.html

LISTS AND LINKS

*Genealogy Mailing Lists for Indiana
members.aol.com/gfsjohnf/gen_mail_states-in.html

Indiana Archival and Historical Repositories
cawley.archives.nd.edu/sia/guide/reposito.htm

*Indiana GenWeb Project
www.rootsweb.com/~ingenweb/

*NUCMC Guide to Indiana Archives and Repositories
lcweb.loc.gov/coll/nucmc/insites.html

———— ••◦◉◦•• ————

IOWA

Iowa Department of Public Health, Des Moines
idph.state.ia.us/pa/vr.htm

Historical Society of Iowa Library and Archives, Des Moines
and Iowa City
www.uiowa.edu/~shsi/library/library.htm

State Library of Iowa, Des Moines
www.silo.lib.ia.us/

Grout Museum of History and Science Library, Waterloo
iowa-counties.com/blackhawk/grout-museum/grout.htm

Iowa Genealogical Society and Library, Des Moines
www.digiserve.com/igs/igs.htm

Iowa State University, Parks Library, Ames
www.iastate.edu/

University of Iowa Library, Iowa City
www2.arcade.uiowa.edu/main/

University of Northern Iowa, Rod Library, Cedar Falls
www.uni.edu/petersog/

INFORMATION SITES

Amana Colonies Web Site
www.jeonet.com/amanas

Iowa Pioneers Project
www.ldyhawk.com/ipl/ipl_main.htm

SELECTED INDEXES AND DOCUMENTS ONLINE

Index to the Women's History Archives at the University
of Iowa Library
www.lib.uiowa.edu/iwa

*Iowa Biographies Project
www.mividaloca.com/IABios/

LISTS AND LINKS

*Genealogy Mailing Lists for Iowa
members.aol.com/gfsjohnf/gen_mail_states-ia.html

*Iowa GenWeb Project
www.rootsweb.com/~iagenweb/iowa.htm

*Links to Iowa Libraries on the Internet
www.scl.ameslab.gov/links/libraries-iowa.html

*NUCMC Guide to Iowa Archives and Repositories
lcweb.loc.gov/coll/nucmc/iasites.html

KANSAS

Kansas Department of Health, Topeka
www.kdhe.state.ks.us/vital/index.html

Kansas State Historical Society, Topeka
history.cc.ukans.edu/heritage/kshs/kshs1.html

Kansas State Library, Topeka
skyways.lib.ks.us/kansas/KSL/

Agricultural Hall of Fame and National Center, Bonner Springs
www.aghalloffame.com/

Bethel College, Mennonite Library and Archives, North Newton
www.bethelks.edu/services/mla/

Bukovina Society of the Americas Museum, Ellis
members.aol.com/LJensen/bukovina.html

Frontier Army Museum, Fort Leavenworth
leav-www.army.mil/museum/

Kansas Genealogical Society Library, Dodge City
www.dodgecity.net/kgs/

Kansas Heritage Center, Dodge City
www.ksheritage.org/

Riley County Genealogical Society Library, Manhattan
history.cc.ukans.edu/heritage/kshs/places/goodnow.htm

University of Kansas Library, Kansas Collection, Lawrence
kuhttp.cc.ukans.edu/cwis/units/kulib/kanscol.html

INFORMATION SITES

Kansas Forts Network
history.cc.ukans.edu/heritage/kshs/places/fortsnet.htm

Kansas Methodist History
history.cc.ukans.edu/heritage/um/um.html

SELECTED INDEXES AND DOCUMENTS ONLINE

Kansas Pioneers Project
history.cc.ukans.edu/heritage/pioneers/pion_main.html

LISTS AND LINKS

*Genealogy Mailing Lists for Kansas
members.aol.com/gfsjohnf/gen_mail_states-ks.html

*Kansas GenWeb Project
skyways.lib.ks.us/genweb/index.html

*NUCMC Guide to Kansas Archives and Repositories
lcweb.loc.gov/coll/nucmc/kssites.html

———— •••❀❀❀••• ————

KENTUCKY

Office of Vital Statistics, Frankfort
www.kdla.state.ky.us/arch/vitastat.htm

*Kentucky Archives and Special Collections
www.louisville.edu/library/uarc/kyarchiv.html

Kentucky Department for Libraries and Archives (KDLA), Frankfort
www.kdla.state.ky.us/

Kentucky Historical Society Library, Frankfort
www.state.ky.us/agencies/khs/research/special_collections1.htm

Kentucky Department of Military Affairs, Military Records and Research
    Branch, Frankfort
www.state.ky.us/agencies/military/mrrb.htm

Blazer Library, Kentucky State University, Frankfort
www.kysu.edu/library/default.html

The Filson Club Historical Society, Louisville
www.filsonclub.org/

Kentucky Genealogical Society, Frankfort
members.aol.com/bdharney2/bh3.htm

Morehead State University, Camden-Carroll Library, Morehead
www.morehead-st.edu/units/library/

Paducah Public Library, Genealogy and Special Collections
www.vci.net/ppl/

Tri-State Genealogical Society, Evansville, Indiana
www.evansville.net/~tsgs/tsgs.html

University of Kentucky, Margaret I. King Library, Lexington
www.uky.edu/Libraries/Special/

Western Kentucky University, Kentucky Library, Bowling Green
www2.wku.edu/library/dlsc/ky_lib.htm

INFORMATION SITES

Dates of the Creation of Kentucky Counties
www.state.ky.us/agencies/khs/research/list_counties.htm

SELECTED INDEXES AND DOCUMENTS ONLINE

Kentucky Vital Records Index
ukcc.uky.edu/~vitalrec/

LISTS AND LINKS

*Genealogy Mailing Lists for Kentucky
members.aol.com/gfsjohnf/gen_mail_states-ky.html

*Kentucky GenWeb Project
www.rootsweb.com/~kygenweb/

*KDLA Links to Other Sites: Genealogy
www.kdla.state.ky.us/links/geneal.htm

*NUCMC Guide to Kentucky Archives and Repositories
lcweb.loc.gov/coll/nucmc/kysites.html

------------ ••◦◉◐◦•• ------------

LOUISIANA

Office of Public Health, Vital Records Registry, New Orleans
www.cdc.gov/nchswww/howto/w2w/louisia.htm

Louisiana State Archives and Records, Baton Rouge
www.sec.state.la.us/arch-1.htm

State Library of Louisiana, Louisiana Section, Baton Rouge
smt.state.lib.la.us/dept/lasect/index.htm

Louisiana Historical Center Library, Louisiana State Museum,
    New Orleans
www.crt.state.la.us/crt/museum/lsmnet3.htm

Louisiana Historical Society, New Orleans
www.acadiacom.net/lahistsoc/

Louisiana Genealogical and Historical Society, Baton Rouge
cust2.iamerica.net/mmoore/lghs.htm

Louisiana State University, Hill Memorial Library, Baton Rouge
www.lib.lsu.edu/special/

New Orleans Public Library, Louisiana Division, New Orleans
home.gnofn.org/~nopl/nutrias.htm

Southwest Louisiana Genealogical Society, Lake Charles
cust2.iamerica.net/nmoore/swlgs.htm

Tulane University, Amistad Research Center, New Orleans
www.arc.tulane.edu/

Tulane University, Howard-Tilton Memorial Library, New Orleans
www.tulane.edu/~lmiller/SpecCollHomePage.html

University of Southwest Louisiana, Louisiana Room, Lafayette
www.usl.edu/Departments/Library/departments/larm.html

INFORMATION SITES

Acadian Genealogy Homepage
www.acadian.org/

Genealogical Materials in the New Orleans Public Library's Louisiana Division and City Archives. 3rd ed. (1996)
home.gnofn.org/~nopl/guides/genguide/ggcover.htm

A Medley of Cultures: Louisiana History at the Cabildo
www.crt.state.la.us/crt/museum/publica.htm

Parishes with Filmed Civil Records at the New Orleans Public Library
and at the FHL
www.gnofn.org/~nopl/guides/genguide/loucivil.htm

SELECTED INDEXES AND DOCUMENTS ONLINE

Bureau of Land Management Land Patent Records Site
www.glorecords.blm.gov/

Louisiana Heritage Network Database
lhn.lsu.edu/lhin/html/entryp.htm

Louisiana Land Records Index
searches.rootsweb.com/cgi-bin/laland/laland.pl

Orleans Parish Court Index to Slave Emancipation Petitions
www.gnofn.org/~nopl/guides/genguide/civcts.htm

Orleans Parish Index to Successions, 1846–1853
www.gnofn.org/~nopl/inv/cdcdemo/menu.htm

LISTS AND LINKS

*Archival Research Repositories in New Orleans
www.tulane.edu/~lmiller/GNOA.html

*Genealogical and Historical Societies in Louisiana
cust2.iamerica.net/mmoore/genlistla.htm

*Genealogy Mailing Lists for Louisiana
members.aol.com/gfsjohnf/gen_mail_states-la.html

Louisiana Clerks of Court
www2.linknet.net/lehman/district.html

*Louisiana GenWeb Project
www.rootsweb.com/~lagenweb/

*NUCMC Guide to Louisiana Archives and Repositories
lcweb.loc.gov/coll/nucmc/lasites.html

———— ••●❂●•• ————

MAINE

Maine Department of Health, Office of Vital Records, Augusta
www.state.me.us/dhs/main/faq.htm

Maine State Archives, Augusta
www.state.me.us/sos/arc/general/admin/mawww001.htm

Maine State Library, Augusta
www.state.me.us/msl/mslhome.htm

Maine Historical Society Research Library, Center for Maine History, Portland
www.mainehistory.com/

Bowdoin College, Hawthorne-Longfellow Library, Brunswick
www.bowdoin.edu/dept/library

Maine Genealogical Society, Farmington
www.rootsweb.com/~megs/MaineGS.htm

Penobscot Maritime Museum, Searsport
www.acadia.net/pmmuseum/

University of Maine at Fort Kent, Acadian Archives
www.umfk.maine.edu/infoserv/archives/welcome.htm

University of Maine at Orono, Folger Library, State of Maine Collections
libraries.maine.edu/orospeccoll/mainecol.htm

INFORMATION SITES

History of the Courts in Maine
www.state.me.us/sos/arc/archives/judicial/courthis.htm

Maine Diary Directory
www.rootsweb.com/~meandrhs/mediary.html

SELECTED INDEXES AND DOCUMENTS ONLINE

Index of Maine Marriages, 1892–1966
thor.ddp.state.me.us/archives/plsql/archdev.Marriage_Archive. search_form

New England Old Newspaper Index Project of Maine
www.geocities.com/Heartland/Hills/1460/

LISTS AND LINKS

*Genealogy Mailing Lists for Maine
members.aol.com/gfsjohnf/gen_mail_states-me.html

*Historical Records Repositories in Maine
www.state.me.us/sos/arc/mhrab/repos/repoweb1.htm

*Links to Maine Libraries
www.state.me.us/msl/melibson.htm

*Maine GenWeb Project
www.rootsweb.com/~megenweb/

*NUCMC Guide to Maine Archives and Repositories
lcweb.loc.gov/coll/nucmc/mesites.html

———————— ••••◦◉◦•••• ————————

MARYLAND

Department of Health, Division of Vital Records, Baltimore
www.cdc.gov/nchswww/howto/w2w/maryland.htm

Maryland State Archives, Hall of Records, Annapolis
www.mdarchives.state.md.us/

Maryland State Law Library, Annapolis
www.lawlib.state.md.us/

Maryland Historical Society, Baltimore
www.mdhs.org/

National Archives at College Park
www.nara.gov/nara/dc/Archives2_info.html

C. Burr Artz Library, Maryland Room, Frederick
www.co.frederick.md.us/fcpl/md-hist.html

Charles County Community College Library, Southern Maryland Studies
    Center, La Plata
www.charles.cc.md.us/library.htm

Maryland Genealogical Society, Baltimore
www.rootsweb.com/~mdsgs/

Enoch Pratt Free Library, Baltimore
www.pratt.lib.md.us/

Talbot County Free Library, Maryland Room, Easton
www.talb.lib.md.us/

University of Maryland at College Park, McKeldin Library,
    Marylandia Collection
www.lib.umb.edu/UMS/UMCP/RARE/797hmpg.html

Washington County Free Library, Western Maryland Room, Hagerstown
pilot.wash.lib.md.us/wcfl/wmr.html

Wicomico County Free Library, Maryland Room, Salisbury
www.co.wicomico.md.us/library/

INFORMATION SITES

Baltimore County Public Libraries Local History Collections
www.bcplonline.org/libpg/libcoll.html#Local

Finding Aids and Indexes at the Maryland State Archives
www.mdarchives.state.md.us/msa/refserv/html/findaid.html

Maryland Immigration Digital Library
www.clis.umd.edu/~mddlmddl/791/frameset.html

SELECTED INDEXES AND DOCUMENTS ONLINE

Indexes to Maryland Marriage References at the Hall of Records
**www.mdarchives.state.md.us/msa/refserv/stagser/ssu1500/html/ssu
    1527.html**

LISTS AND LINKS

*Genealogy Mailing Lists for Maryland
members.aol.com/gfsjohnf/gen_mail_states-md.html

*Maryland GenWeb Project
www.rootsweb.com/~mdgenweb/

*NUCMC Guide to Maryland Archives and Repositories
lcweb.loc.gov/coll/nucmc/mdsites.html

MASSACHUSETTS

Massachusetts Department of Public Health, Registry of Vital Records
  and Statistics, Boston
www.magnet.state.ma.us/dph/vitrecs.htm

Massachusetts Archives, Boston
www.magnet.state.ma.us/sec/arc/arcidx.htm

Massachusetts Historical Society Library, Boston
masshist.org/html/the_library.html

National Archives—Northeast Region (Boston)
www.nara.gov/regional/boston.html

National Archives—Northeast Region (Pittsfield)
www.nara.gov/regional/pittsfie.html

American Antiquarian Society, Worcester
[no http://] **gopher://mark.mwa.org/**

Association for Gravestone Studies, Greenfield
www.berkshire.net/ags/

Berkshire Athenaeum, Pittsfield
www.berkshire.net/~bfha/abtathen.htm

Boston Public Library
www.bpl.org/

Congregational Library and Archives, Boston
www.14beacon.org/

Haverhill Public Library
www.haverhill.com/library/hpl2dept3.html

Library of the Boston Athenaeum
www.bostonathenaeum.org/

Massachusetts Society of Mayflower Descendants, Boston
www.tiac.net/users/msmd/

New England Historic Genealogical Society, Boston
www.nehgs.org/

Plymouth Public Library, Plymouth
idt.net/~ppl1/

Springfield Genealogy and Local History Library at the Quadrangle
www.quadrangle.org/CVHM.htm

University of Massachusetts, Lowell, Center for Lowell History
libvax.uml.edu/~clh/

INFORMATION SITES

Colonial Massachusetts and Maine Genealogy
www.qni.com/~anderson/index.html

Massachusetts Online Library Catalogs
www.mlin.lib.ma.us/catalog.htm

Researching Your Family's History at the Massachusetts Archives
www.state.ma.us/sec/arc/arcfam/famidx.htm

Salem Witch Web Page
www.ogram.org/17thc/salem-witch-list.shtml

SELECTED INDEXES AND DOCUMENTS ONLINE

Ancestry Library's Massachusetts Marriage Index
www.ancestry.com/

Boston Public Library Obituary Database
[no http://] **gopher://bpl.org:70/00gopher_root%3A%5Bspec_coll
%5Dabout_obits_database.doc**

LISTS AND LINKS

*Genealogy Mailing Lists for Massachusetts
members.aol.com/gfsjohnf/gen_mail_states-ma.html

*Massachusetts Cities and Towns Links
www.state.ma.us/cc/

*Massachusetts Library Links
www.mlin.lib.ma.us/homepage.htm

*Massachusetts GenWeb Project
www.rootsweb.com/~magenweb/

*NUCMC Guide to Massachusetts Archives and Repositories
lcweb.loc.gov/coll/nucmc/masites.html

MICHIGAN

Division for Vital Records and Health Statistics, Lansing
www.mdch.state.mi.us/PHA/OSR/vitframe.htm

State Archives of Michigan, Lansing
www.sos.state.mi.us/history/archive/archive.html

Library of Michigan, Lansing
www.libofmich.lib.mi.us/genealogy/genealogy.html

Michigan Historical Center, Lansing
www.sos.state.mi.us/history/history.html

Central Michigan University, Clarke Historical Library, Mount Pleasant
www.lib.cmich.edu/clarke/clarke.htm

Detroit Public Library, Burton Historical Archives
www.detroit.lib.mi.us/special_collections.htm

Flint Public Library
www.flint.lib.mi.us/fpl/resources/genealogy/genealogy.html

Grand Rapids Public Library
www.iserv.net/grpl

Public Libraries of Saginaw, Eddy Historical and Genealogical Collection
www.saginaw.lib.mi.us/eddy.htm

Suomi College, Finnish-American Heritage Center, Hancock
www.suomi.edu/

University of Michigan, Bentley Historical Library, Ann Arbor
www.umich.edu/~bhl/

Western Michigan Genealogical Society, Grand Rapids
www.iserv.net/~wmgs/

Western Michigan University, Archives and Regional History Collection, Kalamazoo
www.wmich.edu/library/archives.html

INFORMATION SITES

Michigan 1895 Atlas
www.livgenmi.com/1895mi

Early Michigan Diaries and Autobiographies
www.libofmich.lib.mi.us/genealogy/midiaries.html

How to Research Your Family at the Library of Michigan
www.libofmich.lib.mi.us/genealogy/researchfamily.html

Michigan Historical Collection at the Bentley Library
www.umich.edu/~bhl/

SELECTED INDEXES AND DOCUMENTS ONLINE

Bureau of Land Management Land Patent Records Site
www.glorecords.blm.gov/

LISTS AND LINKS

*Genealogy Mailing Lists for Michigan
members.aol.com/gfsjohnf/gen_mail_states-mi.html

*Michigan Archival Institutions
h-net2.msu.edu/~maa/archives.html

*Michigan County Clerks' Genealogical Directory
www.sos.state.mi.us/history/archive/archgene.html

*Michigan GenWeb Project
www.rootsweb.com/~migenweb/

*NUCMC Guide to Michigan Archives and Repositories
lcweb.loc.gov/coll/nucmc/misites.html

---

*Indicates URL with links to other sites

MINNESOTA

Minnesota Department of Health, Minneapolis
www.health.state.mn.us/forms.html

Minnesota Historical Society Research Center and Minnesota State
    Archives, Saint Paul
www.mnhs.org/

American Swedish Institute, Minneapolis
www.americanswedishinst.org/

Military History Society of Minnesota, Little Falls
www.dma.state.mn.us/website/cpripley/index.htm

Minneapolis Public Library, Minneapolis Collection
www.mpls.lib.mn.us/

Minnesota Genealogical Society Library, Minneapolis
www.mtn.org/mgs/

Moorhead State University, Northwest Minnesota Historical Center
www.moorhead.msus.edu/~library/

Saint Cloud University, Central Minnesota Historical Center
lrs.stcloud.msus.edu/

Saint Olaf College, Rolvaag Library, Norwegian-American Historical
    Association, Northfield
www.stolaf.edu/stolaf/other/naha/naha.html

University of Minnesota, Duluth, Northeast Minnesota Historical Center
www.d.umn.edu/lib/collections/nemn.html

University of Minnesota, Saint Paul, Immigration History
    Research Center
www.umn.edu/ihrc

INFORMATION SITES

Genealogical Research Sources at the Minnesota Historical Society
www.mnhs.org/research/rg9.htm

Genealogical Resources at the University of Minnesota Libraries
www.lib.umn.edu/reference/genealogy.html

SELECTED INDEXES AND DOCUMENTS ONLINE

Bureau of Land Management Land Patent Records Site
www.glorecords.blm.gov/

Minnesota Obituaries
www.pconline.com/~mnobits/

Minnesota Historical Society Photograph Database
www.mnhs.org/collections/photo/bsearch.html

LISTS AND LINKS

Addresses for Minnesota Regional Research Centers: Central (St. Cloud), Northeast (Duluth), Northwest (Moorhead), Southern (Mankato), Southwest (Marshall), and West Central (Morris)
www.mnhs.org/prepast/mho/regcent.html

*Directory of Minnesota Historical Associations
www.mnhs.org/prepast/mho/mho.html

*Genealogy Mailing Lists for Minnesota
members.aol.com/gfsjohnf/gen_mail_states-mn.html

*Minnesota GenWeb Project
www.rootsweb.com/~mngenweb/

*NUCMC Guide to Minnesota Archives and Repositories
lcweb.loc.gov/coll/nucmc/mnsites.html

———— ••∙◉∙•• ————

MISSISSIPPI

Vital Records, State Department of Health, Jackson
vitalrec.com/ms.html#state

Mississippi Department of Archives and History, Jackson
www.mdah.state.ms.us/

Mississippi Historical Society, Jackson
www.mdah.state.ms.us/mhistsco.html

Mississippi State University, Mitchell Memorial Library, Starkville
nt.library.msstate.edu/

*Indicates URL with links to other sites

University of Mississippi, Archives and Special Collections, University
www.olemiss.edu/depts/south/index.html

University of Southern Mississippi, McCain Library, Hattiesburg
www.lib.usm.edu/mccain.html

INFORMATION SITES

Mississippi Civil War History Sources
www2.msstate.edu/~gam3/cw/

SELECTED INDEXES AND DOCUMENTS ONLINE

Children Taken to Mississippi on the Orphan Train
www.rootsweb.com/~msgenweb/orphan.shtml

Early Southwest Mississippi Territory Pioneer Database
www.rootsweb.com/%7Emsadams/pioneerdb.htm

LISTS AND LINKS

*Genealogy Mailing Lists for Mississippi
members.aol.com/gfsjohnf/gen_mail_states-ms.html

*Mississippi GenWeb Project
www.rootsweb.com/~msgenweb/

*NUCMC Guide to Mississippi Archives and Repositories
lcweb.loc.gov/coll/nucmc/mssites.html

MISSOURI

Missouri Department of Health, Jefferson City
**www.health.state.mo.us/BirthAndDeathRecords/BirthAndDeath
    Records.html**

Missouri State Archives, Jefferson City
mosl.sos.state.mo.us/rec-man/arch.html

Missouri State Library, Jefferson City
mosl.sos.state.mo.us/lib-ser/libser.html

Missouri Historical Society, Saint Louis
library.wustl.edu/~spec/archives/aslaa/

State Historical Society of Missouri, Columbia
www.system.missouri.edu/shs/reference.html

National Archives—Central Plains Region (Kansas City)
www.nara.gov/regional/kansasci.html

National Archives—National Personnel Records Center (Saint Louis)
www.nara.gov/nara/frc/mpromp.html

Genealogical Society of Central Missouri, Columbia
www.coin.missouri.edu/community/genealogy/cent-mo

Kansas City Public Library
www.kcpl.lib.mo.us/

Mid-Continent Public Library, Genealogy and Local History Department, Independence
www.mcpl.lib.mo.us/ge/

Missouri State Genealogical Association, Columbia
www.umr.edu/~mstauter/mosga/

University of Missouri-Columbia, Western Historical Manuscript Collection
www.system.missouri.edu/whmc/

University of Missouri-Kansas City, Western Historical Manuscript Collection
www.umkc.edu:81/whmckc/

University of Missouri-Rolla, Western Historical Manuscript Collection
www.umr.edu/~whmcinfo/

University of Missouri-Saint Louis, Western Historical Manuscript Collection
jinx.umsl.edu/~whmc

INFORMATION SITES

Dates of the Organization of Missouri Counties
mosl.sos.state.mo.us/rec-man/archives/croll1.html

Resources for Family and Community History
mosl.sos.state.mo.us/rec-man/archweb/history.html

SELECTED INDEXES AND DOCUMENTS ONLINE

Bureau of Land Management Land Patent Records Site
www.glorecords.blm.gov/

Kansas City Public Library Local History Database
www.kcpl.lib.mo.us/sc/history/localhistory.htm

LISTS AND LINKS

Directory of Archives and Manuscripts Repositories in the
    Saint Louis Area
library.wustl.edu/~spec/archives/aslaa/directory/

*Genealogy Mailing Lists for Missouri
members.aol.com/gfsjohnf/gen_mail_states-mo.html

*Missouri GenWeb Project
www.rootsweb.com/~mogenweb/mo.htm

*NUCMC Guide to Missouri Archives and Repositories
lcweb.loc.gov/coll/nucmc/mosites.html

MONTANA

Montana Department of Public Health and Human Services, Vital
    Statistics Bureau, Helena
www.cdc.gov/nchswww/howto/w2w/montana.htm

Montana Historical Society Library and Archives, Helena
www.his.mt.gov/

Montana State Library, Helena
msl.mt.gov/

Cascade County Historical Society Archives, Great Falls
www.mtgr.mtlib.org/www/library/cchs.html

Lewiston Public Library/Lewiston Genealogical Society
lewis-carnegie-library.org/

Missoula Public Library
www.montana.com/mslaplib/

Montana State Genealogical Society, Chester
www.rootsweb.com/~mtmsgs/

Montana State University-Billings, Center for the Northern Plains
www.msubillings.edu/northplains/

Montana State University-Bozeman, Burlingame Special Collections
www.lib.montana.edu/collect/spcoll/

University of Montana, Mansfield Library, Missoula
www.lib.umt.edu/

Western Montana College, Lucy Carson Library, Dillon
www.lib.wmc.edu/

INFORMATION SITES

Collections at the Montana Historical Society
his.mt.gov/html/archiv_4.html

Genealogy at the Missoula Public Library
www.montana.com/mslaplib/gen.html

SELECTED INDEXES AND DOCUMENTS ONLINE

Battle of Little Big Horn Casualties
www.rootsweb.com/~usgenweb/mt/mtfiles.htm

Index to *Society of Montana Pioneers*. Vol. 1 (1899)
www.imt.net/~corkykn/pioneer.html

LISTS AND LINKS

*Genealogy Mailing Lists for Montana
members.aol.com/gfsjohnf/gen_mail_states-mt.html

*Montana Archives, Libraries and Historical Societies
www.his.mt.gov/html/archiv_5a.html

*Montana GenWeb Project
www.imt.net/~corkykn/montana.html

*NUCMC Guide to Montana Archives and Repositories
lcweb.loc.gov/coll/nucmc/mtsites.html

NEBRASKA

Nebraska Department of Health and Human Services, Vital Records,
  Lincoln
www.cdc.gov/nchswww/howto/w2w/nebrask.htm

Nebraska State Historical Society, State Archives Division, Lincoln
www.nebraskahistory.org/index.htm

Dana College, Dana Immigrant Archives, Blair
www.dana.edu/~pformo/archive.htm

Grand Island/Edith Abbot Memorial Library
www.gi.lib.ne.us/

Nebraska State Genealogical Society, Lincoln
www.rootsweb.com/~negenweb/societies/stgnsoc.html

Omaha Public Library, Genealogy Department
www.omaha.lib.ne.us/

Stuhr Museum of the Prairie Pioneer, Grand Island
www.gionline.net/arts/stuhr

University of Nebraska, Love Library, Lincoln
www.unl.edu/libr/libs/love.html

INFORMATION SITES

Guide to Genealogical Research at the Nebraska Historical Society
www.nebraskahistory.org/lib-arch/services/refrence/la_pubs/guide
  1.htm

List of Basic Sources on Nebraska History
www.nebraskahistory.org/lib-arch/services/refrence/la_pubs/source
  s4.htm

SELECTED INDEXES AND DOCUMENTS ONLINE

Compendium of History Reminiscence and Biography of Western Nebraska (1909)
www.rootsweb.com/~neresour/NSHS/cofhar/

History of the State of Nevada (1882)
www.ukans.edu/carrie/kancoll/andreas_ne/

LISTS AND LINKS

*Genealogy Mailing Lists for Nebraska
members.aol.com/gfsjohnf/gen_mail_states-ne.html

*Nebraska GenWeb Project
www.rootsweb.com/~negenweb/

*Nebraska Libraries Online
www.nlc.state.ne.us/nelib/nelib.html

*NUCMC Guide to Nebraska Archives and Repositories
lcweb.loc.gov/coll/nucmc/nbsites.html

NEVADA

Division of Health/Vital Statistics, Carson City
vitalrec.com/nv.html

Nevada State Library and Archives, Carson City
www.clan.lib.nv.us/docs/NSLA/ARCHIVES/arc-rec.htm

Nevada State Museum and Historical Society, Las Vegas
www.clan.lib.nv.us/docs/MUSEUMS/LV/mus-lv.htm

Nevada Historical Society, Reno
www.clan.lib.nv.us/

University of Nevada, James R. Dickinson Library, Las Vegas
library.nevada.edu/speccol/index.html

INFORMATION SITES

Central Nevada Emigrant Trail Association, Battle Mountain
ourworld.compuserve.com/homepages/trailofthe49ers/

Nevada State Archives Records and Genealogical Resources
www.clan.lib.nv.us/docs/NSLA/ARCHIVES/geneal.htm

SELECTED INDEXES AND DOCUMENTS ONLINE

Carson Appeal Newspaper Index, 1865–1886 (various years)
www.clan.lib.nv.us/docs/NSLA/ARCHIVES/appeal/appeal.htm

Nevada Newspaper Index Locations
www.clan.lib.nv.us/docs/NSLA/ARCHIVES/newsind.htm

Nevada State Prison Inmate Case Files Index, 1863–1972
www.clan.lib.nv.us/docs/NSLA/ARCHIVES/prison/nsp.htm

LISTS AND LINKS

*Genealogy Mailing Lists for Nevada
members.aol.com/gfsjohnf/gen_mail_states-nv.html

*Nevada GenWeb Project
www.rootsweb.com/~nvgenweb/nvstate.htm

*NUCMC Guide to Nevada Archives and Repositories
lcweb.loc.gov/coll/nucmc/nvsites.html

NEW HAMPSHIRE

Bureau of Vital Records, Concord
www.cdc.gov/nchswww/howto/w2w/newhamp.htm

New Hampshire Division of Records Management and Archives,
  Concord
www.state.nh.us/state/archives.htm

New Hampshire State Library, Concord
webster.state.nh.us/nhsl/index.html

New Hampshire Historical Society Library, Concord
newww.com/org/nhhs

Dartmouth College, Baker Library, Hanover
www.dartmouth.edu/~library

New Hampshire Society of Genealogists, Concord
www.tiac.net/users/nhsog/

University of New Hampshire, Dimond Library, Piscataqua Pioneers
    Program, Durham
wwwsc.library.unh.edu/specoll

INFORMATION SITES

Guide to the New Hampshire State Archives
www.state.nh.us/state/guidemnu.htm

Piscataqua Pioneers Collection
wwwsc.library.unh.edu/specoll/piscapio.htm

SELECTED INDEXES AND DOCUMENTS ONLINE

New Hampshire Historical Society Searchable Collection
nhhistory.org/databases/index.html

LISTS AND LINKS

*Genealogy Mailing Lists for New Hampshire
members.aol.com/gfsjohnf/gen_mail_states-nh.html

*New Hampshire GenWeb Project
www.geocities.com/Heartland/5275/nh.htm

*NUCMC Guide to New Hampshire Archives and Repositories
lcweb.loc.gov/coll/nucmc/nhsites.html

———— ••◦◉◦•• ————

NEW JERSEY

New Jersey State Department of Health, Trenton
www.state.nj.us/health/vital/vital.htm

New Jersey State Archives, Trenton
www.state.nj.us/state/darm/archives.html

New Jersey State Library, Trenton
www.state.nj.us/statelibrary/njlib.htm

New Jersey Historical Society Library, Newark
[no Internet access; Web site under construction, phone 973-596-8500]

Atlantic County Library, New Jersey Collection, Mays Landing
commlink.atlantic.county.lib.nj.us/aclsref.htm

Cape May Historical and Genealogical Society Library, Cape May
    Courthouse
www.beachcomber.com/Capemay/histsoc.html

Drew University, United Methodist Archives, Madison
www.gcah.org/

Gloucester County Historical Society Library, Woodbury
www.rootsweb.com/~njglouce/gchs/

Monmouth County Archives, Manalapan
www.shore.co.monmouth.nj.us/01171_archives/test.htm

Morris County Library, New Jersey Collection, Whippany
www.gti.net/mocolib1/MCL.html

Rutgers University, Special Collections and Archives, New Brunswick
www.libraries.rutgers.edu/rulib/spcol/spcol.htm

Seton Hall University, New Jersey Catholic Historical Records
    Commission, South Orange
www.shu.edu/library/catholicrec/index.html

Trenton Public Library, Trentoniana Department
www.trentonlibrary.state.nj.us/trenton/trenton.html

INFORMATION SITES

New Jersey State Library Frequently-Asked Questions: Genealogy
204.142.36.5/webpac/faqgene.htm

SELECTED INDEXES AND DOCUMENTS ONLINE

New Jersey GenWeb Archives
www.rootsweb.com/~usgenweb/nj/njfiles.htm

LISTS AND LINKS

*Genealogy Mailing Lists for New Jersey
members.aol.com/gfsjohnf/gen_mail_states-nj.html

*New Jersey GenWeb Project
www.cyberenet.net/~gsteiner/njgenweb/

*NUCMC Guide to New Jersey Archives and Repositories
lcweb.loc.gov/coll/nucmc/njsites.html

----------- ••••◉••••• -----------

NEW MEXICO

State of New Mexico Department of Health, Santa Fe
www.state.nm.us/state/doh.html

New Mexico State Records Center and Archives, Santa Fe
www.state.nm.us/

New Mexico State Library, Santa Fe
www.stlib.state.nm.us/

Museum of New Mexico History Library, Santa Fe
lib.nmsu.edu/

Albuquerque Public Library
www.cabq.gov/rgvls/specol.html

Kit Carson Historic Museum, Taos
www.hgrc-nm.org/

Hispanic Genealogical Research Center of New Mexico, Albuquerque
www.hrgc-nm.org/

Historical Society for Southeast New Mexico Museum and Archives,
    Roswell
www.nmculture.org/HTML/southe.htm

New Mexico Genealogical Society, Albuquerque
www.nmgs.org/

New Mexico State University, Rio Grande Historical Collections,
    Las Cruces
[no http://] **gopher://lib.nmsu.edu:70/11/.aboutlib/.archives**

Santa Fe Trail Historical Society, Springer
www.nmculture.org/HTML/northc.htm

Silver City Local History Research Library
www.zianet.com/silverweb/museum/index.html

Southern New Mexico Genealogical Society, Las Cruces
www.zianet.com/wheelerwc/GenSSNM/

University of New Mexico, Center for Southwest Research, Albuquerque
www.unm.edu/~cswrref/

INFORMATION SITES

History of New Mexico
www.newmexico.org/culture/history.html

New Mexico State University Genealogy Resources
lib.nmsu.edu/guides/other/geneal

SELECTED INDEXES AND DOCUMENTS ONLINE

Great New Mexico Pedigree Database
www.hgrc.nm.org/surnames/surnames.htm#Surnames

LISTS AND LINKS

*Genealogy Mailing Lists for New Mexico
members.aol.com/gfsjohnf/gen_mail_states-nm.html

*New Mexico GenWeb Project
www.rootsweb.com/~nmgenweb/

New Mexico Library Directory
www.stlib.state.nm.us/zianet.html

*NUCMC Guide to New Mexico Archives and Repositories
lcweb.loc.gov/coll/nucmc/nmsites.html

———————— ••••••••• ————————

NEW YORK

New York State Department of Public Health, Albany
www.health.state.ny.us/nysdoh/consumer/vr.htm

[for vital records, see also:]
Municipal Archives of the City of New York
www.ci.nyc.ny.us/html/doris/html/archives.html

New York State Archives, Albany
unix6.nysed.gov/default.htm

New York State Library, Albany
www.nysl.nysed.gov/

New-York Historical Society Library, New York
www.nyhistory.org/

New York State Historical Association Research Library, Cooperstown
cooperstown.net/nysha/#Library

National Archives—Northeast Region (New York City)
www.nara.gov/regional/newyork.html

Adriance Memorial Library, Poughkeepsie
midhudson.org/member/adriance.html

American Baptist Historical Society, Rochester
www.crds.edu/abhs.htm

Brooklyn Public Library, Brooklyn Collection
www.brooklynpubliclibrary.org/central/brcoll.htm

East Hampton Free Library, Long Island Collection
www.peconic.net/easthampton/library/

Ellis Island Museum, American Family Immigration Center
www.ellisisland.org/

Montgomery County Department of History and Archives, Fonda
www.superior.net/~emogen34/other_org/history.htm

New York Genealogical and Biographical Society, New York
www.nygbs.org/

New York Public Library, U.S. History, Local History, and Genealogy
Division, New York
www.nypl.org/

Queens Borough Public Library, Long Island Division
www.queens.lib.ny.us/special/longisland.html

Rochester Public Library
www.rochester.lib.ny.us/

INFORMATION SITES

Genealogical Sources at the New York State Archives
unix6.nysed.gov/holding/fact/genea-fa.htm

Local Records on Film at the New York State Archives
unix6.nysed.gov/holding/fact/local-mi.htm

SELECTED INDEXES AND DOCUMENTS ONLINE

Albany County Naturalization Records Index
www.albanycounty.com/achor

Ellis Island Wall of Honor Database
www.wallofhonor.com/wallofhonor/search_f.asp

Probate Indexes for New York Counties
www.wasatch.com/~dsam/sampubco/newyork.htm

LISTS AND LINKS

*Genealogy Mailing Lists for New York
members.aol.com/gfsjohnf/gen_mail_states-ny.html

Guide to Local History and Archives Collections in the Genessee Valley
www.rrlc.org/guide/

List of New York County Clerks
www.dos.state.ny.us/lists/coclerks.html

*New York GenWeb Project
www.rootsweb.com/~nygenweb/

*NUCMC Guide to New York Archives and Repositories
lcweb.loc.gov/coll/nucmc/nysites.html

————— ••◦◉◦•• —————

NORTH CAROLINA

North Carolina Department of Health and Human Services, Vital
   Records Section, Raleigh
www.schs.state.nc.us/SCHS

North Carolina Division of Archives and History, Raleigh
www.ah.dcr.state.nc.us/

State Library of North Carolina, Raleigh
statelibrary.dcr.state.nc.us/NCSLHOME.HTM

Duke University, William R. Perkins Library, Durham
www.lib.duke.edu/

East Carolina University, Joyner Library, Greenville
www.ecu.edu/

North Carolina Genealogical Society, Raleigh
www.ncgenealogy.org/

Rowan County Public Library, Salisbury
www.lib.co.rowan.nc.us/

University of North Carolina at Chapel Hill, Wilson Library
www.lib.unc.edu/wilson/index.html

INFORMATION SITES

African-American Documentary Resources in North Carolina
www.upress.virginia.edu/epub/pyatt/index.html

Genealogical Research in North Carolina
statelibrary.dcr.state.nc.us/iss/gr/genealog.htm

SELECTED INDEXES AND DOCUMENTS ONLINE

North Carolina GenWeb Military Archives
www.rootsweb.com/~usgenweb/nc/military.htm

LISTS AND LINKS

*Genealogy Mailing Lists for North Carolina
members.aol.com/gfsjohnf/gen_mail_states-nc.html

*North Carolina GenWeb Project
www.rootsweb.com/~ncgenweb/

*NUCMC Guide to North Carolina Archives and Repositories
lcweb.loc.gov/coll/nucmc/ncsites.html

NORTH DAKOTA

North Dakota Department of Health, Bismarck
www.ehs.health.state.nd.us/ndhd/admin/vital

State Historical Society of North Dakota, North Dakota Heritage Center,
 Bismarck
www.state.nd.us/hist/

Germans from Russia Heritage Society, Bismarck
grhs.com/

North Dakota State University Library, North Dakota Institute for
 Regional Studies, Fargo
www.lib.ndsu.nodak.edu/ndirs

Red River Valley Genealogical Society Library, Fargo
www.atpfargo.com/hjem/rrvgs/index.html

University of North Dakota, Chester Fritz Library, Grand Forks
www.und.nodak.edu/dept/library/Collections/spk.html

INFORMATION SITES

Institute for Regional Studies Biography and Genealogy Collections
www.lib.ndsu.nodak.edu/ndirs/bio&genealogy/index.html

North Dakota Pioneer Biography Files
www.lib.ndsu.nodak.edu/ndirs/bio&genealogy/pioneerbiofiles.html

SELECTED INDEXES AND DOCUMENTS ONLINE

1885 Dakota Territory Census Index
www.state.nd.us/hist/infcens.htm

Fargo Forum Obituary Database
www.lib.ndsu.nodak.edu/ndirs/bio&genealogy/forumobits.html

North Dakota Biography Index
www.lib.ndsu.nodak.edu/ndirs/bio&genealogy/ndbioindex.html

North Dakota Naturalization Records Database
www.lib.ndsu.nodak.edu/ndirs/bio&genealogy/ndnatrecords.html

LISTS AND LINKS

*Genealogy Mailing Lists for North Dakota
members.aol.com/gfsjohnf/gen_mail_states-nd.html

*North Dakota GenWeb Project
www.rootsweb.com/~ndgenweb/

*NUCMC Guide to North Dakota Archives and Repositories
lcweb.loc.gov/coll/nucmc/ndsites.html

*Regional-Genealogical and Historical Society Addresses
**www.lib.ndsu.nodak.edu/ndirs/bio&genealogy/reggen&histaddres
ses.html**

OHIO

Ohio Department of Health, Columbus
www.odh.state.oh.us/

State Library of Ohio, Columbus
winslo.ohio.gov/index.html

Ohio Historical Society, Columbus
www.ohiohistory.org/index.html

Bluffton College, Mennonite Historical Library, Bluffton
library.norweld.lib.oh.us/Bluffton

Bowling Green State University, Jerome Library, Bowling Green (Ohio
   Network of American History Research Centers)
www.bgsu.edu/colleges/library/cac/cac.html

Cincinnati-Hamilton Public Library
plch.lib.oh.us/

Oberlin College Library, Oberlin
www.oberlin.edu/~library/

Ohio Genealogical Society, Mansfield
www.ogs.org/

Ohio State University, William O. Thompson Memorial Library,
   Columbus
www.lib.ohio-state.edu/

Ohio University Archives, Athens (Ohio Network of American History
   Research Centers)
www.library.ohiou.edu/

University of Akron Library (Ohio Network of American History
   Research Centers)
www.uakron.edu/library/

University of Cincinnati Library (Ohio Network of American History
   Research Centers)
www.libraries.uc.edu/

Wayne County Public Library, Wooster
library.norweld.lib.oh.us/Wayne/

Western Reserve Historical Society, Cleveland (Ohio Network of
   American History Research Centers)
www.wrhs.org/

Wright State University, Dunbar Library, Dayton (Ohio Network of
American History Research Centers)
www.wright.edu/

Youngstown Historical Center of Industry and Labor (Ohio Network of
American History Research Centers)
winslo.ohio.gov/ohswww/youngst/arch_lib.html

INFORMATION SITES

Genealogical Resources at the State Library of Ohio
www.ohiohistory.org/resource/archlib/

History of the Western Reserve
www.infinet.com/~dzimmerm/western.html

Ohio Genealogy: A Step-by-Step Guide
www.infinet.com/~dzimmerm/mgenhow2.html

SELECTED INDEXES AND DOCUMENTS ONLINE

Bureau of Land Management Land Patent Records Site
www.glorecords.blm.gov/

Miami Valley Genealogical Index
www.pcdl.lib.OH.US/miami/miami.htm

Ohio Death Certificate Index, 1913–1927, 1933–1937
www.ohiohistory.org/dindex/search.cfm

Ohio Query Surname Index
www.rootsweb.com/~ohfrankl/Free/queries.htm

War of 1812 Roster of Ohio Soldiers
www.ohiohistory.org/resource/database/rosters.html

LISTS AND LINKS

*Genealogy Mailing Lists for Ohio
members.aol.com/gfsjohnf/gen_mail_states-oh.html

*NUCMC Guide to Ohio Archives and Repositories
lcweb.loc.gov/coll/nucmc/ohsites.html

*Ohio GenWeb Project
www.rootsweb.com/~ohgenweb/

*Ohio Network of American History Research Centers (Akron, Bowling
    Green, Cincinnati, Cleveland, Columbus, Dayton, and Youngstown)
www.ohiohistory.org/textonly/resource/lgr/networkl.html

OKLAHOMA

Oklahoma State Department of Health, Oklahoma City
www.health.state.ok.us/

Office of Archives and Records, Oklahoma Department of Libraries,
    Oklahoma City
www.odl.state.ok.us/oar/

Oklahoma Historical Society, Oklahoma City
www.keytech.com/~frizzell/ohspage.html

Cherokee Heritage Center, Tahlequah
www.powersource.com/powersource/heritage/center.html

Museum of the Great Plains, Lawton
www.sirinet.net/~mgp/page4.html

Oklahoma Genealogical Society, Oklahoma City
www.rootsweb.com/~okgs/

Oklahoma State University Library, Stillwater
www.library.okstate.edu/index.htm

Will Rogers Memorial Library, Claremore
www.willrogers.org/

Southwest Oklahoma Genealogical Society, Lawton
www.sirinet.net/~lgarris/swogs/

University of Oklahoma, Western History Collections, Norman
www-lib.ou.edu/depts/west/index.htm

University of Tulsa, McFarlin Library
www.utulsa.edu/

INFORMATION SITES

So Your Grandmother Was a Cherokee Princess?
www.powersource.com/powersource/cherokee/gene.html

SELECTED INDEXES AND DOCUMENTS ONLINE

Case File Enrollment Records of the Five Civilized Tribes
www.nara.gov/nara/searchnail.html [enter "enrollment records five
    civilized tribes" in search field]

Index to Applications for Eastern Cherokee Roll of 1909
www.nara.gov/nara/searchnail.html [enter "Guion Miller Roll" in search
    field]

LISTS AND LINKS

*Directory of Oklahoma Public Libraries
www.odl.state.ok.us/go/pl.asp

*Genealogy Mailing Lists for Oklahoma
members.aol.com/gfsjohnf/gen_mail_states-ok.html

*NUCMC Guide to Oklahoma Archives and Repositories
lcweb.loc.gov/coll/nucmc/oksites.html

*Oklahoma GenWeb Project
www.rootsweb.com/~okgenweb/okindex.htm

*Oklahoma Indian Territory GenWeb Project
www.rootsweb.com/~itgenweb/

OREGON

Oregon Center for Health Statistics, Portland
www.ohd.hr.state.or.us/cdpe/chs/certif/certfaqs.htm

Oregon State Archives, Salem
arcweb.sos.state.or.us/default.html

Oregon State Library, Salem
www.osl.state.or.us/oslhome.html

Oregon Historical Society Library, Portland
www.ohs.org/homepage.html

Genealogical Forum of Oregon, Inc., Portland
www.gfo.org/

Oregon Genealogy Society, Springfield
www.rootsweb.com/~genepool/ogsinfo.htm

Southern Oregon Historical Society Library, Medford
www.sohs.org/

INFORMATION SITES

Genealogy Records at the State Archives
arcweb.sos.state.or.us/geneal.html

Guide to Provisional and Territorial Records
arcweb.sos.state.or.us/provisionalguide/provisionaltable.html

Historical County Records Guide
arcweb.sos.state.or.us/county/cphome.html

SELECTED INDEXES AND DOCUMENTS ONLINE

Oregon Pioneer Biographies
www.rootsweb.com/~orgenweb/pioneerbios.html

Oregon State Archives Genealogical Name Database
159.121.115.13/databases/searchgeneal.html

LISTS AND LINKS

*Genealogy Mailing Lists for Oregon
members.aol.com/gfsjohnf/gen_mail_states-or.html

*NUCMC Guide to Oregon Archives and Repositories
lcweb.loc.gov/coll/nucmc/orsites.html

*Oregon GenWeb Project
www.rootsweb.com/~orgenweb/

*Oregon Library Links
www.open.org/ola/oregon-libraries.html

PENNSYLVANIA

Pennsylvania Department of Health, Division of Vital Records,
New Castle
www.state.pa.us/PA_Exec/

Pennsylvania State Archives, Harrisburg
www.state.pa.us/PA_Exec/Historical_Museum/DAM/psa.htm

State Library of Pennsylvania, Harrisburg
www.cas.psu.edu/docs/pde/LIBCOLL.HTML

Historical Society of Pennsylvania, Philadelphia
www.libertynet.org/pahist/

National Archives—Mid Atlantic Region (Philadelphia)
www.nara.gov/regional/philacc.html

Allentown Public Library
www.allentownpl.org/

American Swedish Historical Museum, Philadelphia
www.libertynet.org/ashm/

Balch Institute for Ethnic Studies, Philadelphia
www.libertynet.org/balch/

Berks County Historical Society Library, Reading
www.berksweb.com/histsoc/

Bucks County Historical Society Library, Doylestown
www.libertynet.org/bchs/

Carnegie Library of Pittsburgh
www.clpgh.org/clp/

Civil War Library & Museum, Philadelphia
www.libertynet.org/cwlm/

David Library of the American Revolution, Washington Crossing
www.libertynet.org/dlar/dlar.html

Free Library of Philadelphia
www.library.phila.gov/

Genealogical Society of Pennsylvania, Philadelphia
www.libertynet.org/gspa/

Germantown Historical Society Library, Philadelphia
www.libertynet.org/ghs/

Grand Army of the Republic War Museum and Library, Philadelphia
suvcw.org/garmus.htm

Haverford College, Magill Library, Haverford
www.haverford.edu/

Senator John Heinz Pittsburgh Regional History Center
www.pghhistory.org/

Montgomery County Historical Society, Norristown
www.innernet.net/hively/HistSocYork.htm

Philadelphia City Archives
www.phila.gov/phils/carchive.htm

Presbyterian Historical Society, Philadelphia
www.libertynet.org/pacscl/phs/

Swarthmore College, Friends Historical Library, Swarthmore
www.swarthmore.edu/

Temple University Libraries, Philadelphia
www.temple.edu/speccoll/

University of Pennsylvania Library, Philadelphia
www.library.upenn.edu/

U.S. Army Military History Institute, Carlisle Barracks
carlisle-www.army.mil/usamhi/

York County Archives, York
www.york-county.org/about/archives.htm

INFORMATION SITES

Beginner's Guide to Pennsylvania State Land Records
www.state.pa.us/PA_Exec/Historical_Museum/DAM/landrec.htm

Bibliography of Pennsylvania in the American Revolution
www.army.mil/cmh-pg/reference/revbib/pa.htm

Genealogical Research in the Published Pennsylvania Archives
www.cas.psu.edu/docs/pde/libgen.html

Record Groups at the Pennsylvania State Archives
www.state.pa.us/PA_Exec/Historical_Museum/DAM/rg/

State Library of Pennsylvania Records of Interest to Genealogists
www.cas.psu.edu/docs/pde/libgenrec.html

SELECTED INDEXES AND DOCUMENTS ONLINE

Beers Biographical Record Online
www.chartiers.com/beers-project/beers.html

Pennsylvania Archives Index
www.rootsweb.com/~usgenweb/pa/pafiles.htm

LISTS AND LINKS

*Genealogical and Historical Organizations in Pennsylvania
www.libertynet.org/gencap/pagenorg.html

*Genealogy Mailing Lists for Pennsylvania
members.aol.com/gfsjohnf/gen_mail_states-pa.html

*NUCMC Guide to Pennsylvania Archives and Repositories
lcweb.loc.gov/coll/nucmc/pnsites.html

*Pennsylvania GenWeb Project
www.libertynet.org/gencap/pacounties.html

RHODE ISLAND

Rhode Island State Department of Health, Division of Vital Records,
    Providence
www.cdc.gov/hchswww/howto/w2w/rdisland.htm

Rhode Island State Archives, Providence
[no http://] **gopher://archives.state.ri.us/**

Rhode Island State Library, Providence
www.sec.state.ri.us/library/web.htm

Rhode Island Historical Society, Providence
[no Internet access, phone 401-331-8575]

American-French Genealogical Society, Woonsocket
users.ids.net/~afgs/afgshome.html

Brown University, John Hay Library, Providence
**www.brown.edu/Facilities/University_Library/general/libraries/hay
    .html**

Cranston Historical Society
www.geocities.com/Heartland/4678/sprague.html

Providence Public Library, Rhode Island Collection
www.provlib.org/srrcweb.htm

Redwood Library and Athenaeum, Newport
www.redwood1747.org/special1.htm

Warwick Public Library, Greene Collection
users.ids.net/warwickpl/home.htm

Woonsocket Harris Public Library, Woonsocket
www.ultranet.com/~whpl/

INFORMATION SITES

Rhode Island Reading Room
www.rootsweb.com/~rigenweb/articles.html

SELECTED INDEXES AND DOCUMENTS ONLINE

Rhode Island GenWeb Archives
www.rootsweb.com/usgenweb/ri/risearch.html

LISTS AND LINKS

*Directory of Rhode Island Public Libraries
www.lori.state.ri.us/lori/libraries/pubdir1.htm

*Genealogy Mailing Lists for Rhode Island
members.aol.com/gfsjohnf/gen_mail_states-ri.html

*NUCMC Guide to Rhode Island Archives and Repositories
lcweb.loc.gov/coll/nucmc/risites.html

*Rhode Island GenWeb Project
www.rootsweb.com/~rigenweb/

*Rhode Island Town Links
www.athena.state.ri.us/info/city.htm

SOUTH CAROLINA

South Carolina Department of Health and Human Services, Columbia
www.dhhs.state.sc.us/

South Carolina Department of Archives and History, Columbia
www.state.sc.us/scdah/

South Carolina State Library, Columbia
www.state.sc.us/scsl/index.html

South Carolina Historical Society, Charleston
www.schistory.org/

Avery Research Center for African American History & Culture of the
College of Charleston
www.cofc.edu/library/avery/avery.html

Charleston County Library, South Carolina Room, Charleston
www.ccpl.org/scr.html

South Carolina Genealogical Society, Greenville
www.geocities.com/Heartland/Woods/2548

University of South Carolina, South Caroliniana Library, Columbia
www.sc.edu/library/socar/

Winthrop University, Dacus Library, Rock Hill
www.winthrop.edu/dacus/archives.html

INFORMATION SITES

Counties in South Carolina, Bibliographies
www.state.sc.us/scsl/sources.html

Genealogical Research at the South Carolina Department of Archives
    and History
www.state.sc.us/scdah/genealre.htm

SELECTED INDEXES AND DOCUMENTS ONLINE

South Carolina Marriage Records, 1641–1799
www.rootsweb.com/~usgenweb/sc/sca_marr.html

South Carolina Historical Society 20,000 Surname Guide
www.historic.com/schs/gbrowse/browse.html

LISTS AND LINKS

*Genealogy Mailing Lists for South Carolina
members.aol.com/gfsjohnf/gen_mail_states-sc.html

*NUCMC Guide to South Carolina Archives and Repositories
lcweb.loc.gov/coll/nucmc/scsites.html

*South Carolina GenWeb Project
www.geocities.com/Heartland/Hills/3837

SOUTH DAKOTA

Department of Health, Vital Statistics, Pierre
www.state.sd.us/state/executive/doh/

South Dakota State Archives, Pierre
www.state.sd.us/state/executive/deca/cultural/archives.htm

South Dakota State Historical Society, Pierre
www.state.sd.us/state/executive/deca/cultural/sdshs.htm

Augustana College, Mikkelsen Library, Center for Western Studies,
    Sioux Falls
inst.augie.edu/CWS/

High Plains Heritage Center, Spearfish
www.state.sd.us/tourism/adds/highpla.htm

South Dakota Genealogical Society, Pierre
www.rootsweb.com/~sdgenweb/gensoc/sdgensoc.html

South Dakota State University, Brookings
www.sdstate.edu/li11/http/arch.html

University of South Dakota, I.D. Weeks Library, Spearfish
www.usd.edu/library/special

INFORMATION SITES

Genealogy Resources at the South Dakota State Archives
www.state.sd.us/state/executive/deca/cultural/arc_gene.htm

South Dakota History Chronology
www.state.sd.us/state/executive/deca/cultural/soc_hist.htm

South Dakota Oral History Index
www.usd.edu/iais/oralhist/index.html

Study and Timeline of the Lakota Nation
www-personal.umich.edu/~jamarcus/

SELECTED INDEXES AND DOCUMENTS ONLINE

Rosebud Reservation Marriage Licenses, 1906–9, 1915 (brides)
ftp.rootsweb.com/pub/usgenweb/sd/native/rb-bride.txt

Rosebud Reservation Marriage Licenses, 1906–9, 1915 (grooms)
ftp.rootsweb.com/pub/usgenweb/sd/native/rb-groom.txt

South Dakota Ancestors Database
www.rootsweb.com/~sdgenweb/ancestors/ancindex.html

LISTS AND LINKS

*Genealogy Mailing Lists for South Dakota
members.aol.com/gfsjohnf/gen_mail_states-sd.html

*NUCMC Guide to South Dakota Archives and Repositories
lcweb.loc.gov/coll/nucmc/sdsites.html

*South Dakota GenWeb Project
www.rootsweb.com/~sdgenweb/

TENNESSEE

Tennessee Department of Health, Nashville
www.state.tn.us/health/vr/

Tennessee State Library and Archives, Nashville
www.state.tn.us/other/statelib/tslahome.htm

East Tennessee History Center, Knoxville
www.korrnet.org/knoxlib/ethc.htm

East Tennessee State University, Sherrod Library, Archives of Appalachia,
Johnson City
www.etsu-tn.edu/library/sherrod.htm

Middle Tennessee State University Library, Tennessee Collection,
Murfreesboro
frank.mtsu.edu/~library/

Southern Baptist Historical Library and Archives, Nashville
www.sbhla.org/

Tennessee Genealogical Society Library, Memphis
www.rootsweb.com/~tngs/

INFORMATION SITES

Genealogical Fact Sheets on Tennessee Counties
www.state.tn.us/sos/statelib/pubsvs/intro.htm

Genealogical Research in the University of Tennessee Library
www.lib.utk.edu/collect/library_guides/guide_030.pdf

SELECTED INDEXES AND DOCUMENTS ONLINE

Index to Tennessee Legislative Acts, 1796–1850
www.state.tn.us/sos/statelib/pubsvs/actindex.htm

Index to Soldiers Home Applications
www.state.tn.us/sos/statelib/pubsvs/csh_intr.htm

Partial Index to Tennessee Death Records, 1914–1925
www.state.tn.us/sos/statelib/pubsvs/death.htm

Southern Claims Commission Applications, 1871–1873
www.state.tn.us/sos/statelib/pubsvs/sccintro.htm

LISTS AND LINKS

*Genealogy Mailing Lists for Tennessee
members.aol.com/gfsjohnf/gen_mail_states-tn.html

Network of Tennessee County Historians
www.state.tn.us/sos/statelib/pubsvs/historns.htm

*NUCMC Guide to Tennessee Archives and Repositories
lcweb.loc.gov/coll/nucmc/tnsites.html

*Tracking Your Roots (Tennessee)
members.aol.com/TYR%20Lisa/tyrtenn.htm

*Tennessee GenWeb Project
www.rootsweb.com/~tngenweb.org/

TEXAS

Texas Department of Health, Austin
www.tdh.state.tx.us/

Texas State Library and Archives, Austin
www.tsl.state.tx.us/

Texas General Land Office, Austin
www.glo.state.tx.us/

Texas State Historical Association, Austin
www.tsha.utexas.edu/

National Archives-Southwest Region (Fort Worth)
www.nara.gov/regional/ftworth.html

Stephen F. Austin State University, Center for East Texas Studies, Nacogdoches
www.cets.sfasu.edu/

Catholic Archives of Texas, Austin
www.onr.com/user/cat/

Daughters of the Republic of Texas Library, San Antonio
www.drtl.org/

Historical Society of Denton County, Denton
www.iglobal.net/mayhouse/dentonhistorypage.html

Houston Public Library, Clayton Library for Genealogical Research
sparc.hpl.lib.tx.us/hpl/clayton.html

San Antonio Central Library, Texana/Genealogy Department
www.sat.lib.tx.us/html/genealog.htm

Harold B. Simpson Confederate Research Center, Hillsboro
www.texashf.org/publications/sum96/scrapbook9607.html

Southern Methodist University, De Goyler Library and Methodist Historical Library, Dallas
www.smu.edu/~swcenter/

Texas Seaport Museum, Galveston
www.phoenix.net/~tsm

Texas State Genealogical Society, Carrollton
www.rootsweb.com/~txsgs/tsgs.html

University of Texas at Austin, Center for Studies in Texas History
www.tsha.utexas.edu/

University of Texas at Austin, Center for American History
www.lib.utexas.edu/Libs/CAH/

University of Texas at El Paso Library, Special Collections
libraryweb.utep.edu/speccoll/default.html

University of Texas at San Antonio Library
www.lib.utsa.edu/index.html

West Texas A&M University, Panhandle-Plains Historical Museum,
Canyon
www.wtamu.edu/museum/

INFORMATION SITES

County Records on Film at the Texas State Library and Archives
www.tsl.state.tx.us/lobby/local/locrmenu.htm

Genealogy Research at the Texas State Archives
www.tsl.state.tx.us/lobby/arcgen.htm

General Land Office Finding Aids
www.glo.state.tx.us/central/arc/findaid.html

New Handbook of Texas (1996)
www.tsha.utexas.edu/handbook/index.html

SELECTED INDEXES AND DOCUMENTS ONLINE

Confederate Pension Applications Index, 1899–1964
link.tsl.state.tx.us/c/compt/index.html

"Old 300" Database of Austin Colony Land Grants
www.tgn.net/~bchm/Genealogy/gene.html

Republic of Texas Military Rolls Index, 1835–1845
www.mindspring.com/~dmaxey/

Texas Adjutant General Service Records Index, 1836–1935
www.tsl.state.tx.us/lobby/servrecs.htm

LISTS AND LINKS

*Genealogy Mailing Lists for Texas
members.aol.com/gfsjohnf/gen_mail_states-tx.html

*NUCMC Guide to Texas Archives and Repositories
lcweb.loc.gov/coll/nucmc/txsites.html

*Texas GenWeb Project
www.rootsweb.com/~txgenweb/

*Texas History Online
www.tsha.utexas.edu/history-online/index.html

UTAH

Utah Bureau of Vital Records, Salt Lake City
hlunix.state.ut.us/bvr/home.html

Utah State Archives and Record Services, Salt Lake City
www.archives.state.ut.us/

Utah State Library, Salt Lake City
www.state.lib.ut.us/

Utah State Historical Society, Salt Lake City
www.ce.ex.state.ut.us/history/

Brigham Young University, Harold B. Lee Library, Provo
library.byu.edu/newhome.html

Family History Library of the Church of Jesus Christ of Latter-day
    Saints, Salt Lake City
www.lds.org/

University of Utah, Marriott Library, Salt Lake City
www.lib.utah.edu/index.phtml

Utah Genealogical Association, Salt Lake City
www.infouga.org/

Utah State University, Merrill Library Special Collections, Logan
www.usu.edu/~specol/index.html

INFORMATION SITES

Collections and Documents on Utah History
www.ce.ex.state.ut.us/history/collect.htm

Guide to Archives and Manuscript Collections in Selected Utah Repositories
    (1989)
www.ce.ex.state.ut.us/history/utahguid.htm

Heritage Birth Certificates
hlunix.state.ut.us/bvr/html/heritage.html

SELECTED INDEXES AND DOCUMENTS ONLINE

Utah Cemeteries Burials Database
rdbms.utah.org:204/

Utah History Encyclopedia
eddy.media.utah.edu/medsol/UCME/UCMEFRAMES/index.html

LISTS AND LINKS

*Genealogy Mailing Lists for Utah
members.aol.com/gfsjohnf/gen_mail_states-ut.html

*NUCMC Guide to Utah Archives and Repositories
lcweb.loc.gov/coll/nucmc/utsites.html

*Utah GenWeb Project
www.lofthouse.com/USA/Utah/

VERMONT

Vermont Department of Health, Vital Records Section, Burlington
www.ahs.state.vt.us/

Vermont State Archives, Montpelier
www.sec.state.vt.us/archives/archdex.htm

Vermont Historical Society, Montpelier
www.state.vt.us/vhs/

Bennington Museum Genealogy/History Library
www.bennington.com/museum/gene.html

Brooks Memorial Library, Brattleboro
www.state.vt.us/libraries/b733/brookslibrary

Genealogical Society of Vermont, Saint Albans
ourworld.compuserve.com/homepages/induni_n_J/homepage.htm

University of Vermont, Bailey/Howe Memorial Library, Burlington
moose.uvm.edu/~edow/wilbur.html

Vermont French-Canadian Genealogical Society Library, Burlington
members.aol.com/vtfcgs/genealogy/index.html

INFORMATION SITES

*Genealogical Research in Vermont
www.state.vt.us/vhs/generes.htm

Guide to Records at the Vermont State Archives
vermont-archives.org/guide/aguide.htm

SELECTED INDEXES AND DOCUMENTS ONLINE

Vermont GenWeb Archives
www.rootsweb.com/~usgenweb/vt/vtfiles.htm

LISTS AND LINKS

*Genealogy Mailing Lists for Vermont
members.aol.com/gfsjohnf/gen_mail_states-vt.html

*NUCMC Guide to Vermont Archives and Repositories
lcweb.loc.gov/coll/nucmc/vtsites.html

Vermontania Collections (directory)
www.uvm.edu/~histpres/vtiana/vccont.html

*Vermont GenWeb Project
www.rootsweb.com/~vtgenweb/vtgenweb.htm

VIRGINIA

Virginia Department of Health, Richmond
www.vdh.state.va.us/

Library of Virginia, Richmond
leo.vsla.edu/lva.html

Virginia Historical Society, Richmond
www.vahistorical.org/

Thomas Balch Library, Leesburg
leo.vsla.edu/reposit/sites/tbl.html

Bureau of Land Management, Eastern States, Springfield
www.blm.gov/

College of William and Mary, Earl Gregg Swem Library, Williamsburg
www.swem.wm.edu/

Colonial Williamsburg Foundation Library, Williamsburg
www.history.org/

Eastern Mennonite University, Menno-Simons Historical Center, Harrisonburg
www.emu.edu/library/lib.htm

Handley Regional Library, Winchester
www.shentel.net/handley-library/index.html

Mariner's Museum, Newport News
www.mariner.org/library.html

Memorial Foundation of the Germanna Colonies, Culpeper
www.summit.net/germanna

Museum of the Confederacy, Richmond
www.moc.org/

National Genealogical Society, Arlington
www.ngsgenealogy.org/

United Daughters of the Confederacy, Richmond
www.hqudc.org/

University of Virginia, Alderman Library, Charlottesville
www.lib.virginia.edu/index.html

Virginia Genealogical Society, Richmond
www.vgs.org/

Virginia Military Institute Archives, Lexington
www.vmi.edu/~archtml/index.html

*Indicates URL with links to other sites

Mary Ball Washington Museum and Library, Lancaster
leo.vsla.edu/reposit/sites/mbwm.html

INFORMATION SITES

Guide to Civil War Materials in the Swem Library
www.swem.wm.edu/SPCOL/CivilWar/webcw2.html

*Library of Virginia Genealogy Home Page
leo.vlsa.edu/archives/genie.html

VA-NOTES (series on Virginia documents)
leo.vsla.edu/vanotes/

Virtual Library of Virginia
scholar2.lib.vt.edu/spec/viva/viv.htm

SELECTED INDEXES AND DOCUMENTS ONLINE

Confederate Navy Electronic Card Index
198.17.62.51/collections/CN.html

Confederate Rosters Electronic Card Index
198.17.62.51/collections/CF.html

Henley Marriage and Obituary Database
eagle.vsla.edu/henley/

Index of Confederate Veterans' and Widows' Pension Rolls, 1888–1934
198.17.62.51/collections/CW.html

Index to War of 1812 Muster Rolls and Payrolls
eagle.vsla.edu/war1812/

Index to Wills and Administrations (Torrence)
eagle.vsla.edu/torrence/

Land Office Patents and Grants Document Images and Surname Index
198.17.62.51/collections/LO.html

Land Office, Northern Neck Grants Document Images and Surname
Index
198.17.62.51/collections/NN.html

Marriage Records Electronic Card Index
198.17.62.51/collections/MG.html

Mexican War Soldiers Electronic Card Index
198.17.62.51/collections/MX.html

Newspapers in Virginia Database
eagle.vsla.edu/newspaper/

Richmond Enquirer and *Richmond Visitor* Marriage Index
198.17.62.51/collections/MI.html

Richmond Enquirer and *Richmond Visitor* Obituary Index
198.17.62.51/collections/OI.html

LISTS AND LINKS

*Directory of Virginia Repositories
leo.vsla.edu/reposit/reposit.html

*Directory of Virginia Libraries
leo.vsla.edu/directory/

*Directory of Virginia Historical Societies
leo.vsla.edu/reference/hisindex.html

*Genealogy Mailing Lists for Virginia
members.aol.com/gfsjohnf/gen_mail_states-va.html

*NUCMC Guide to Virginia Archives and Repositories
lcweb.loc.gov/coll/nucmc/vasites.html

*Virginia GenWeb Project
www.rootsweb.com/~vagenweb/

WASHINGTON

Washington Department of Health, Olympia
www.doh.wa.gov/topics/chs-cert.html

Washington State Archives, Olympia (there are branches of the State
Archives in Bellingham, Cheney, Ellensburg, and Seattle)
www.wa.gov/sec/archives/main.htm

Washington State Archives, Central Region, Ellensburg
www.cwu.edu/~archives

Washington State Library, Washington Northeast Collection, Olympia
www.statelib.wa.gov/

Washington State Historical Society, Heritage Resource Center, Olympia
www.wshs.org/text/mus_res.htm#3

Washington State Historical Society Research Center, Tacoma
www.whsh.org/text/mus_res.htm#1

National Archives—Pacific Alaska Region (Seattle)
www.nara.gov/regional/seattle.html

Seattle Municipal Archives
www.ci.seattle.wa.us/leg/clerk/archhome.htm

Seattle Public Library
www.spl.org/

Tacoma Historical Society
www.powerscourt.com/ths/

Tacoma Public Library
www.tpl.lib.wa.us/

University of Washington, Allen Library, Seattle
www.lib.washington.edu/Suzzallo/

Washington State Genealogical Society, Olympia
www.rootsweb.com/~wasgs/

Washington State University, Holland Library, Pullman
www.wsulibs.wsu.edu/holland/masc/masc.htm

INFORMATION SITES

Genealogical Sources at the Washington State Archives Central
    Region Branch
www.cwu.edu/~archives/genie.htm

SELECTED INDEXES AND DOCUMENTS ONLINE

Index for *Sketches of Washingtonians* (1906)
www.rootsweb.com/~wagenweb/sketch07.htm

Pacific Northwest Regional Newspaper and Periodical Index
www.lib.washington.edu/specialcoll/pnw_current/regional.html

Washington Newspaper Index
192.211.20.10:81/

Washington Placenames Database
www.tpl.lib.wa.us/nwr/placecgi.htm

LISTS AND LINKS

*Genealogy Mailing Lists for Washington
members.aol.com/gfsjohnf/gen_mail_states-wa.html

*NUCMC Guide to Washington Archives and Repositories
lcweb.loc.gov/coll/nucmc/wasites.html

*State of Washington Regional Archives System
www.wa.gov/sec/archives/branches.htm

*Washington GenWeb Project
www.rootsweb.com/~wagenweb/

*Washington Libraries Online
www.walib.spl.org/

WEST VIRGINIA

Vital Registration Office, Charleston
www.cdc.gov/nchswww/howto/w2w/westva.htm

West Virginia Historical Society, West Virginia Division of Culture and
History, Archives and History Section, Charleston
www.wvlc.wvnet.edu/history/wvsamenu.html

West Virginia Historical Society, Charleston
www.wvlc.wvnet.edu/history/wvhssoc.html

Indicates URL with links to other sites

Allegheny Regional Family History Society
www.swcp.com/~dhickman/arfhs.html

Central West Virginia Genealogy & History Library, Horner
www.rootsweb.com/~hcpd/library.htm#central

Greenbrier Historical Society, North House Museum, Lewisburg
web.mountain.net/~ghs/ghs.html

Marshall University, Morrow Library, Huntington
www.marshall.edu/speccoll/wvcoll.html

Ohio County Public Library, Wheeling Room, Wheeling
129.71.122.114/main/wheelrm.htm

West Virginia University Library, Morgantown
www.wvu.edu/~library/

INFORMATION SITES

County Records on Film at the West Virginia State Archives
www.wvlc.wvnet.edu/history/bluenote.html

*Guide to Local History and Genealogy Holdings the Special Collections
Department, James E. Morrow Library, Marshall* (1994)
www.marshall.edu/speccoll/title.html

Mining Your History Federation
www.rootsweb.com/~myhf/

SELECTED INDEXES AND DOCUMENTS ONLINE

Ohio River Valley Families Genealogy Database
orvf.com/

West Virginia Surname Exchange
www.wvlc.wvnet.edu/history/surintro.html

LISTS AND LINKS

*Collections Pertaining to West Virginia Outside of West Virginia
www.wvlc.wvnet.edu/history/reposits_not_wv/states.html

*Genealogy Mailing Lists for West Virginia
members.aol.com/gfsjohnf/gen_mail_states-wv.html

*NUCMC Guide to West Virginia Archives and Repositories
lcweb.loc.gov/coll/nucmc/wvsites.html

*West Virginia GenWeb Project
www.rootsweb.com/~wvgenweb/

*West Virginia History on the Internet
www.wvlc.wvnet.edu/history/wvhs1021.html

*West Virginia Repositories and Historical Societies
www.wvlc.wvnet.edu/history/guide2.html

WISCONSIN

Wisconsin State Department of Health and Family Services, Madison
www.dhfs.state.wi.us/

State Historical Society of Wisconsin, Archives Division, Madison, Area
Research Center (ARC)
www.wisc.edu/shs-archives/

State Historical Society of Wisconsin Library, Madison
www.wisc.edu/shs-library/

Wisconsin Veterans Museum Research Center, Madison
badger.state.wi.us/agencies/dva/museum/research.html

Milwaukee Public Library
www.mpl.org/

Northland College, Dexter Library, Ashland (ARC)
www.wisc.edu/shs-archives/arcnet/northlan.html

Superior Public Library (ARC)
www.wisc.edu/shs-archives/arcnet/superior.html

University of Wisconsin, Eau Claire, McIntyre Library (ARC)
www.wisc.edu/shs-archives/arcnet/eauclair.html

University of Wisconsin, Green Bay, Cofrin Library (ARC)
www.wisc.edu/shs-archives/arcnet/greenbay.html

University of Wisconsin, LaCrosse, Murphy Library (ARC)
www.wisc.edu/shs-archives/arcnet/lacrosse.html

University of Wisconsin, Madison, Max Kade Institute for German-
   American Studies
www.wisc.edu/mki/

University of Wisconsin, Milwaukee, Library (ARC)
www.wisc.edu/shs-archives/arcnet/milwauke.html

University of Wisconsin, Oshkosh, Polk Library (ARC)
www.wisc.edu/shs-archives/arcnet/oshkosh.html

University of Wisconsin, Parkside, Parkside Library (ARC)
www.wisc.edu/shs-archives/arcnet/parkside.html

University of Wisconsin, Platteville, Karmann Library (ARC)
www.wisc.edu/shs-archives/arcnet/plattvil.html

University of Wisconsin, River Falls, Davee Library (ARC)
www.wisc.edu/shs-archives/arcnet/riverfls.html

University of Wisconsin, Stevens Point, Learning Resources Center
www.wisc.edu/shs-archives/arcnet/stevens.html

University of Wisconsin, Stout, Library Learning Center, Menomonie
www.wisc.edu/shs-archives/arcnet/stout.html

University of Wisconsin, Whitewater, Pierce Library (ARC)
www.wisc.edu/shs-archives/arcnet/whitewtr.html

Vesterheim Genealogical Center and Naesth Library, Madison
www.library.wisc.edu/local/memorial/libraries/Memorial/vesterhe.htm

Wisconsin State Genealogical Society, Monroe
www.rootsweb.com/~wsgs/index.htm

INFORMATION SITES

1853 Wisconsin Gazetteer
www.umdl.umich.edu/cgi-bin/moa/sgml/moa-idx?notisid= AFK4346

Illustrated History of the State of Wisconsin
www.umdl.umich.edu/cgi-bin/moa/sgml/moa-idx?notisid= AFK4349

Wisconsin Newspapers
www.n-net.com/wi.htm

SELECTED INDEXES AND DOCUMENTS ONLINE

Bureau of Land Management Land Patent Records Site
www.glorecords.blm.gov/

German Nobility Database
www8.informatik.uni-erlangen.de/cgi-bin/wwp/LANG%3Dgerm/?1

Wisconsin Directory of Ethnic Organizations Database
www.150years.state.wi.us/events/ethn.htm

LISTS AND LINKS

*Area Research Centers for Wisconsin Counties (in Eau Claire, Green
    Bay, LaCrosse, Milwaukee, Oshkosh, Parkside, Platteville, River
    Falls, Stevens Point, Stout, Superior, and Whitewater)
www.wisc.edu/shs-archives/arcnet/index.html

*Genealogy Mailing Lists for Wisconsin
members.aol.com/gfsjohnf/gen_mail_states-wi.html

*NUCMC Guide to Wisconsin Archives and Repositories
lcweb.loc.gov/coll/nucmc/wisites.html

*Wisconsin GenWeb Project
www.rootsweb.com/~wigenweb/

WYOMING

Wyoming Department of Health, Vital Records Services, Cheyenne
wdhfs.state.wy.us/vital_records/default.htm

Wyoming State Archives, Wyoming State Historical Society, Cheyenne
commerce.state.wy.us/CR/Archives/

Wyoming State Library, Cheyenne
www-wsl.state.wy.us/

Buffalo Bill Historical Center Research Library, Cody
www.truewest.com/BBHC/library.htm

Laramie County Library, Cheyenne
library.cheyenneweb.com/

Saratoga Museum of Saratoga
members.xoom.com/kaikin/welcome/

University of Wyoming, American Heritage Center, Laramie
www.uwyo.edu/ahc/

INFORMATION SITES

Chronology of Wyoming History
www.state.wy.us/state/wyoming_news/general/chronology.html #chr

General Facts About Wyoming
www.state.wy.us/state/wyoming_news/general/history.html

Wyoming County Records at the State Archives
commerce.state.wy.us/cr/archives/county/county.htm

SELECTED INDEXES AND DOCUMENTS ONLINE

Index to Yellowstone Archives Master Inventory
www.nps.gov/yell/archives.htm

LISTS AND LINKS

*Genealogy Mailing Lists for Wyoming
members.aol.com/gfsjohnf/gen_mail_states-wy.html

*NUCMC Guide to Wyoming Archives and Repositories
lcweb.loc.gov/coll/nucmc/wysites.html

*Wyoming Libraries Links
www-wsl.state.wy.us/wyld/libraries/index.html

*Wyoming GenWeb Project
www.rootsweb.com/~wygenweb/

ADDITIONAL READING AND RESEARCH

For researching on the Internet, please consult "Organizing Your Online Research," by Marthe Arends, an article in *Online Pioneers* 33 (May 1998): 2–5. Sample articles from *Online Pioneers* can be read at **www.eskimo.com/~mnarends/**. For searching online, the single-most comprehensive site of links for genealogists is *Cyndi's List of Genealogy Sites on the Internet* (**www.cyndislist.com**), a web site maintained by Cyndi Howells, author of *Netting Your Ancestors: Genealogical Research on the Internet* (Baltimore: Genealogical Publishing Company, 1997). For specialized information on working at specific web sites, see books such as *Prima's Official Companion to Family Tree Maker Version 5.0* (Rocklin, CA: Prima Publishing, 1998) by Myra Vanderpool Gormley for information about www.familytreemaker.com.